DE MONTFORT UNIVERSITY LIBRARY
CITY CAMPUS

Enquiry Desk Telephone Numbers

ISSUE/RENEW	257 7043
GENERAL	257 7042
BUSINESS, TECHNICAL AND LAW	257 7044
ART, DESIGN AND BUILT ENVIRONMENT	257 7047

Please return this book on or before the last date stamped
below.

Fines will be charged on books returned after this date.

PC28

FRENCH MUSIC OF TO-DAY

TO

TONY AND MADELEINE GUÉRITTE

A TRIBUTE TO THE
SOCIÉTÉ DES CONCERTS FRANCAIS
AND A TOKEN OF MY
BROTHERLY AFFECTION

FRENCH MUSIC
OF TO-DAY

By
G. JEAN-AUBRY

WITH A PREFACE BY
GABRIEL FAURÉ

TRANSLATED BY EDWIN EVANS

BOOKS FOR LIBRARIES PRESS
PLAINVIEW, NEW YORK

First Published 1919
Reprinted 1976

Library of Congress Cataloging in Publication Data

Jean-Aubry, Georges, 1882-1950.
  French music of to-day.

  "Articles or lectures."
  Translation of La musique française d'aujord'hui.
  Reprint of the 1919 ed., issued in series: Library
of music and musicians.
  1. Music, French. 2. Musicians, French.
I. Title. II. Series: Library of music and
musicians.
ML60.J4213 1973   781.7'44   72-10600
ISBN 0-8369-7113-2

PRINTED IN THE UNITED STATES OF AMERICA

TRANSLATOR'S PREFACE

THE untiring activities of M. G. Jean-Aubry in fostering international amenities in literary, artistic, and musical circles have made his name familiar not only in France and England, but throughout Western Europe. The official mission with which he has recently been entrusted by the French Government is no more than a just recognition of a course of action upon which he had already been privately engaged for many years, and which he would doubtless have continued without such recognition. Primarily his mission has been to spread the knowledge of French achievements in these spheres not only abroad but at home, for even Frenchmen were at first slow to realise the importance of the rejuvenation that had taken place in all the arts during the concluding decades of the nineteenth century. But the same curiosity that led him to the study of recent French achievements was bound eventually to extend itself to corresponding movements in other countries with which his missionary work had brought him into relations. He thus became a sympathetic student first of our poets and then of our musicians, and he is an enthusiastic advocate, not only of contemporary French composers, but of those English, Spanish, and Italian composers whose works place them in the vanguard of present-day music. Thus it comes about that he, a Frenchman, is warmly furthering the claims of modern English music in Spain, Italy, and in other countries. In short, he occupies an international position whose usefulness is enhanced by his unusual breadth of outlook.

He was born in Paris on August 13th, 1882, educated at a provincial *lycée*, and originally destined for a business career, but, even before liberating himself from such ties, he had already embarked upon the work which was subsequently to absorb all his energies. He first attracted attention as the leading spirit in the " Cercle de l'Art Moderne " at Havre, which organised concerts devoted to the works of Claude Debussy, Vincent d'Indy, Paul Dukas, Florent Schmitt, Ernest Chausson, Maurice Ravel, Déodat de Sévérac, and Albert Roussel, most of whom were associated with the performances ; exhibitions of paintings by Monet, Renoir, Matisse, Pissarro, and others of the advanced group ; finally, lectures on Baudelaire, Verlaine, Mallarmé, Laforgue, and other modern poets, most of which he delivered himself. It is in the musical section of this undertaking that will be found the germ of the Société des Concerts Français, by means of which his brother-in-law, M. T. J. Guéritte, has done so much to further the knowledge of modern French music in England.

Subsequently the Town Council of Havre commissioned him to give two series of lectures, in 1910 and 1911, the first of which dealt with " The Evolution of Modern French Poetry from Baudelaire to Francis Jammes," and the second with a few prose writers, including Anatole France, Villiers de l'Isle Adam, Rémy de Gourmont, Jules Renard, Elémir Bourges, André Gide, and Paul Claudel. It is characteristic of him that he selects for preference names which are still under discussion rather than those whose claims are universally admitted. He has the instincts of a pioneer.

Meanwhile he had lectured in France and abroad on the relations between poetry and music as exemplified in Baudelaire and Verlaine. He has appeared at several universities and has been awarded the title of honorary professor by the Université Nouvelle of Brussels. In 1912 the Société des Gens de Lettres awarded him the prize " de la Critique Indépendante."

His interest in England, which he looks upon as a second home, is by no means limited to music. In 1905 he translated Arthur Symons's " The Symbolist Movement in Literature," and he has since rendered into French a number of poems by Swinburne, Ernest Dowson, and Arthur Symons. He has also translated Joseph Conrad's " Within the Tides " and several stories by George Moore. At the same time he has, by means of patient research, collected a mass of interesting particulars concerning the long sojourn of Paul Verlaine in England, and established the date of the poems written in this country, as well as the localities which inspired them. He has also been the first to give in France concerts of modern Spanish music, and among the first to acclaim the interesting musical manifestations of the modern spirit in Italy.

The work of M. G. Jean-Aubry can thus in no sense be regarded as animated by chauvinism. He is a resolute champion of the free exchange of artistic ideas between all nations, believing that therein lies the surest protection against intellectual domination by any one of them. He is the enemy of all exclusiveness, and has played an active part in arousing the curiosity of his own countrymen in the artistic life of other nations.

His book on modern French music represents an accumulation from several years of missionary work. It is far from complete, but he has preferred to place it on record in its present form, the only addition made since the outbreak of war being the first chapter, for which there was an actual need. The appearance of the volume early in the war was due partly to considerations arising out of the war itself, and partly to a very natural desire, with which I have good reason to sympathise, to show that his interest in French music is not of yesterday. Since August, 1914, so many who were hitherto apathetic or even hostile have suddenly declared themselves enthusiastic, that it is really necessary to make some distinction between pioneers and these converts of the eleventh hour.

In spite of the unfavourable conditions, the book has met with considerable success, having run through two French editions, besides appearing in a Spanish translation with a cordial introduction by the most prominent of the younger Spanish composers, M. Manuel de Falla. For the purpose of the English edition it has been necessary to omit the poetic essay entitled " Les Sortilèges des Soirs," which cannot be rendered into English owing to the number of allusions, and to substitute in abridged form a recent paper on the appreciation of modern French music in England.

It is because my own admiration for modern French music is of equally long date, and because I also have been associated with spreading its appreciation, that I regarded it as a personal compliment to be asked to undertake the translation of M. G. Jean-Aubry's book. The difficulties have been unusually great. Though never under any illusion concerning the intricate problem of rendering French prose into English, I was under the impression, before undertaking this volume, that a knowledge of the language made the task easier. Long before concluding my labours that opinion was reversed. The more intimately I understood the author's point of view, the more hopeless it seemed to give it adequate expression through another medium. The implements of M. G. Jean-Aubry's illuminating criticism consist in a number of finely shaded epithets between which it is extremely difficult to differentiate in English. As if that were not enough, there is a subtle significance in the manner in which he groups them, and even in the order in which they are placed. They are, as it were, the colours on his palette, and his brush flits from one to another with a nicety which would require all the resources of paraphrase to do it justice. How I have longed for the easy method that is content to take the nearest word in the dictionary ! But it was denied to me by my own familiarity with the subject treated. If, in the following pages, there remain Gallicisms which it would have been better to Anglicise more completely, and if some of M. Aubry's extended periods would have been more easily read if broken into short sentences, I can only plead in extenuation the effort I have made to reproduce as nearly as possible the characteristics of his critical method and of his literary style. In comparison, the rendering of French idioms is a minor difficulty, and its solution ultimately a matter of taste. I have left " les deux manches et la belle " in the original, translated literally " prendre la lune avec les dents," and rendered by analogy " prendre des vessies pour des lanternes," and can give no better reason in each case than taste and expediency. It is for others to say how far I have succeeded in my primary object of making accessible to English readers a valuable contribution to the literature of a subject which has long been of absorbing interest to me.

My enthusiasm for modern French music is now of twenty years' standing, and, in view of the analogies which so many critics have detected between Musorgsky and Debussy, it is worth recalling that I first became acquainted with the French movement through the Russian composers. The circumstances may perhaps be of some interest. On page 9 of the present volume M. Aubry records an " irresistible and definite sensation of the decadence of German music," which he received on hearing Strauss's " The Legend of Joseph." With me that impression is of much longer date, and it was preceded by a period of scepticism concerning the finality of the ideals even of the German classics who preceded the decadence. I was vaguely conscious of something lacking in them which had been present in the music of the seventeenth and eighteenth centuries, and at the same time I was alertly conscious of a hiatus between those ideals and the German spirit, with which I had come into contact in the most impressionable years of my boyhood. I realised the nobility of the sentiment, but suspected the accompanying eloquence, and was not disposed to accept it without question, as I experienced a difficulty in reconciling it with what I felt concerning both music and Germany. Needless to say, I was regarded almost as a blasphemer. It was at this time that I first heard of Borodin. Very little of his music was then procurable in London, except by order, and I was not in a position to purchase his complete works without knowing more about them, but I became acquainted with a French enthusiast who was more fortunate. This was M. E. Duval-Yzelen, a gifted musician, and the brother of M. Raymond-Duval, the author of the best French edition of Schumann's songs. This gentleman possessed practically the whole of Borodin's works in the form of arrangements for piano duet. We played the volume through from cover to cover. I believe it was at a single sitting, for we had Gargantuan appetites in those days. (On one occasion we played through in the same afternoon the whole of " Hansel and Gretel " and Glazunoff's three-act ballet " Raymonda.") This feast of Borodin was the starting-point of my activities on behalf of modern Russian and French music in turn, for I found in certain portions of this composer's work not only an emancipation from Germany such as one does not meet with, for instance, in either Dvorak or Tchaikovsky, but also that other element, difficult to define, which the romantic movement had gradually submerged in the nineteenth century. In short, Borodin, and Musorgsky when I began to study him, held for me at least the promise that what I had thought to be lacking since the eighteenth century was not lost beyond recall. It was a little later, but still in the late nineties, that the same musical friend, to satisfy my curiosity whether similar movements could be traced elsewhere, played me, as having an affinity with Borodin, the slow movement of Debussy's string quartet, and also prepared me for the appearance of " Pelléas et Mélisande," of which he had private knowledge. Thanks to this valuable hint, I secured a copy— probably one of the first to reach this country—of that masterpiece the moment the original edition was published by M. Fromont. Meanwhile I had not only obtained practically everything that Debussy had in print at that date, but also extended my studies of French music in general. At first it was a slow process, for the more closely I approached the subject the bigger it became, and, M. Duval-Yzelen having returned to France, there was no information obtainable near at hand ; for in those days English musicians still considered Saint-Saëns

the last word in French music. However, soon
after the appearance of " Pelléas " I had the assistance, for which I could never be too grateful, of M.
Vincent d'Indy, the head of the Schola Cantorum,
who not only increased my knowledge but also gave
me some illuminating hints that enabled me to
bring my impressions, which then threatened to
become chaotic owing to the profusion of material,
into some sort of order. Other help reached me
from M. Ed. Moullé, whose wonderful volume of
French folk-songs is another charming acquaintance
I owe to my fortunate meeting with M. Duval-
Yzelen. From that moment my task was easy, and
it was not long before I endeavoured by means of
lectures and articles to draw the attention of
English musicians to the musical treasures lying
neglected at their very doors. Of course I had
the experience of being told, again and again, that
this was not music, and I have some amusing
recollections of the way in which the accompanying
illustrations were received; but as most of my
hecklers, especially since August, 1914, have discovered that all good music does not come from
Germany, it is time to turn the page, with apologies
to the reader for these personal musings.

M. G. Jean-Aubry's book is a considered tribute
to a movement which has restored to France a
characteristic mode of musical expression after an
era of Rossini and Meyerbeer, not to speak of others.
Like the Russian Nationalist movement which
preceded it, but from which it differed in some
essential particulars, this movement should be of

engrossing interest to all those who wish to see
English music set free from the influences which
have so long obstructed its true progress. Of
course it is not the method, but the motives, of the
French composers which should furnish the example
where one is needed. It is not by adding this or
that technical device to the musician's vocabulary
that freedom of expression is to be obtained. There
has already been far too much assimilation of
features which are purely external to French music.
Neither does a set purpose of conscious revolution
promise the best results. Independence does not
consist in mere negation; it is a positive quality, but
it rests ultimately on the responsibility of the artist
and on that alone. The weakness of traditional
methods consists largely in the short cuts to achievement which they lay open to composers of indolent
inventiveness. The strength of the modern French
school resides largely in its scorn of these short cuts.
Few indeed of the modern French composers permit
themselves to have recourse to devices the effect of
which is a foregone conclusion. Were one of their
works lost, one could not restore it, as one could
many pages of German music, from a fragment, like
a naturalist restores an extinct quadruped from a
single bone. They preserve their allegiance to each
individual composition on which they are engaged.
This artistic probity expresses itself in a strict
economy of means and its natural concomitant, the
cleanest precision. Lavishness of means and
opaqueness of texture are the expedients by which
banalities are made pretentious, as Richard Strauss

has proved many times. Economy is the enemy of all such imposture. As Sir Thomas Beecham pointed out in a recent speech, the French composers, by their remarkable sense of précision, are able to sustain the musical interest with the simplest means, and where these answer their purpose they use no more. In this respect they have brought the twentieth century into line with the eighteenth. Allowing for the development which has meanwhile taken place in the musical vernacular, there is little to choose for clarity between Mozart and Ravel. It is this lucidity that we must learn to appreciate if we are to undo the mischief resulting from our saturation with music which does not include this quality among its ideals. Music has more to gain from directness and conciseness than from any assumption of profundity, and it has yet to be proved that either quality is an obstacle to the expression of the noblest thoughts or sentiments. That is what M. G. Jean-Aubry implies in his constant attacks upon over-emphasis.

It is, however, possible to become too exclusive in this appreciation of fine chiselling. It is no more logical to neglect Michael Angelo because one is fascinated by Cellini than it is to despise Cellini because of the grandeur of Michael Angelo. There is, in fact, a remarkable duality in all Western art which has its explanation in the historical origin of the great nations of the West, and, if I may hazard a criticism, M. G. Jean-Aubry is apt sometimes to forget, in his championship of the exquisite, that the same France which achieved perfect expression in

minute poetic forms, such as the rondel, was also
the architect of Rheims cathedral. France is
Gothic as well as Romance, Frankish as well as
Roman, and this duality, which has its equivalent in
England no less than in Italy, plays an important
part in her artistic expression. It is not without
significance that César Franck was an immigrant
from the North, and that the outward appearance of
Debussy was typically Southern. The tendency
that one occasionally observes in French criticism
to regard the Franckist movement, now led by one
of the greatest of French musicians, M. Vincent
d'Indy, as something imported, and not entirely
French, involves a negation of some of the most
vital features in French art. The controversy that
raged in the first decade of the present century
between the champions of two different kinds of
music was never a contest between the national
tradition and foreign influences, but belonged to the
" growing pains " of a vigorous and youthful
movement which had not realised that its *langue
d'oil* and its *langue d'oc* were different aspects of one
language. The national temperament will inevitably
react against excess, whether in emphasis or merely
in dimensions, but that does not exclude the
grandiose from French music any more than the
majesty of symphonic form can be a menace to the
delicacy of the musical miniature. It is beyond the
Rhine that the obsession of size can be observed in
its most characteristic form. It is German criticism,
or criticism based on German ideas, which cannot
admit that a work of art can be great without being

big, but it would be lamentable if the inevitable reaction went so far as to foster the opposite illusion that it must needs be minute. It is at least an interesting theory that German megalomania owes something to the Asiatic infiltration which replenished the partial void created by the westward migration of all that was best in the Teutonic tribes. Shortly before the war a French illustrated journal gave, side by side, photographs of the Arc de Triomphe and of the monument recently erected to commemorate the battle of Leipsig, and the comparison accentuated the barbaric character of the latter, which might have been the landmark of some Babylonian devastator. The Byzantinism of modern Germany is not indigenous to Western Europe.

These are fundamentally matters of taste, in respect of which surely none will deny the right of the French to their own standard. For alertness and finesse they are constantly compared to the Athenians, and the parallel loses none of its force if one extends it to Marathon and the Marne, where the conflict, material and moral, was the same. I would go further, and claim that the emancipation of their music is one of many symptoms that, if rightly understood, would have prepared the world for the magnificent spectacle of 1914, for the doctrine of self-reliance remains the same, whatever its mode of expression, and music is not a side-issue, but an integral feature of national life. Our nation is less articulate, and one would not expect a similar manifestation to make itself felt with equal vividness among us, but the recent renascence of interest in our own music, and the emancipated outlook of our composers during the past twenty years, belong to the same class of phenomena.   It did not need the actual crisis to show that there was a new spirit in England.

Whether one definitely associates this new spirit in France and England with what is known in music as nationalism is beside the point.   It is something more subtle than the nationalism of Russia, consequently less dependent upon such assistance as may be derived from the intensive cult either of folk-song or of native classics.   Even among the Latin nations the English movement presents a much closer analogy with what has taken place in France than with either the Spanish movement as represented by Pedrell, Granados, and Albeniz, or the interesting group of Italian composers headed by Casella, Malipiero, and their companions.   Despite their ancient culture, the Spaniards, like the Russians, had practically clear ground upon which to build, and the Italians had to resist a native rather than a foreign despotism, that of their own operatic tradition.   The problem of the French was to purge their music of parasitical elements, not so much because their origin was foreign in the geographical sense as because they were unsuited to reflect the French mentality, and our own problem is the same in an aggravated form, because the parasitical elements have held longer and more complete sway over our music.   It is not to be solved by the deliberate adoption of mechanical expedients, or even by conscious effort, but only by the subconscious search for more applicable means of expression; and in this search, however different its results may and must be, the French have been our forerunners and are our companions. Hence the mutual esteem which has grown up between French and English musicians is neither fortuitous nor due to statesmanship. It is a natural effect of similar causes operating on both sides of the Channel. It is the task of Frenchmen such as M. Aubry and M. Guéritte, and of Englishmen sharing their views, not so much to create these ties, which grow naturally from existing affinities, as to give them outward expression, and secure for them the recognition of the French and English public.

So far as this country is concerned, little remains to be done. M. Aubry himself confesses that there is no country, out of France, where contemporary French music is so well known and appreciated. I wish we could say the same concerning English music in France, but if that is not yet possible it is for reasons which give no ground for reproach. The French musical public has given ample proof of its receptivity by the prompt appreciation it has given to many modern movements, from that of the Russians to that of the Hungarians, Bartok and Kodaly, on the eve of war. If our music has not made the same headway it is due to two causes. The first is that until recently the element of freshness and independence was not prominent. Frenchmen welcomed Russian music because it gave them something new, which English music in those days did not. *We* might feel that our composers were breaking away from the German tradition, but the differentiation was scarcely perceptible to audiences that were less eager in their search for it. French musicians came expectant and went away with an impression of having heard echoes, faint, maybe, but still echoes, of the Rhine. The second cause of their lack of enthusiasm was that in many cases we sent them the wrong music. A wise missionary studies his audience in the selection of his texts, and there is a wide difference between an English and a Latin audience. This difference was vividly brought home to me a few years ago in connection with a certain concerto which had its first performance in Paris and in London within a few weeks. The work was a product of sound musicianship, not without a certain distinction, but lengthy and somewhat pretentious. The Paris audience, after listening courteously for a little while, expressed its displeasure in a form which brought the performance to a close. The English audience received it with apparent cordiality. I quote the incident to show that there is a psychological difference that must be taken into consideration. I do not wish to imply that the English works performed in Paris have merited the same description, but we have not sufficiently considered, when selecting works for performance abroad, which aspect of our music is most likely to gain acceptance. Our music is, in fact, like our race, made up of many strands, Celtic, Latin, and Teutonic. There is an aspect of it which will be appreciated in Copenhagen, Rotterdam, or Zurich, and utterly rejected in Paris or Rome. It is our misfortune that this aspect for a long time predominated over the others. But the conditions have changed, and there are many works in our repertoire which have a much better prospect of acceptance among the Latins. From the first it is these that should have been put forward in Paris, but such was the strength of reaction that they had to fight strenuously for acceptance at home. Here again the analogy with French experience is a striking one. All of M. Aubry's heroes, or at least their friends on their behalf, have had a hard struggle to secure recognition in their own country. They write and speak in the highest terms of the aid and encouragement they derived from their reception in England. That they were anxious to repay the debt is proved by the fact that they and their friends attended in force M. Guéritte's concerts of English music in Paris, whereas English professional musicians were at first not a conspicuous element at his French concerts in London. The ground is well prepared, but in appraising the progress that has been made it must not be forgotten that the English movement is at the very least a decade younger. If French appreciation of our music follows at the same interval, France will be doing as much for England as England for France. That brings us to the present day, and I have every reason to state with confidence that, so soon as the conditions in Paris permit of it, English works will be sure of a welcome there. But there will still remain the problem of selection. There are living English composers whose works, though estimable in themselves, and highly thought of at home, would only delay French appreciation. Let them find other worlds to conquer, and come to Paris when Paris is better able to judge to what extent they are representative. We have been unfortunate in the past, and may be again if misdirected zeal is allowed to have its way.

One of the most encouraging signs of the times is the system of co-operation that has grown up between important musical associations in Paris, Madrid, and Rome, each with its provincial connections. There is a constant exchange of communications between men who have a finger on the pulse of musical life in each of these countries, and that fosters the mutual introduction of new works. It is in each case the man on the spot who decides what works are likely to be appreciated. This triangular arrangement is capable of indefinite extension, and the process has already begun. At the moment of writing I have just received a programme recording the performance at Turin of works by John Ireland, Eugene Goossens, and Cyril Scott. Several English works are set down for performance in Rome under the auspices of the " Società Italiana di Musica Moderna." Others have been played in Madrid. If there is not similar news from Paris it is only because of conditions which may have changed even before these lines appear in print. Our own record is not in question. We have always thrown open our concert-rooms, perhaps with too little discrimination, to the music of the entire world. The foundations of musical internationalism, as distinct from the former world empire, are laid.   We need perhaps a little more enthusiasm for the principle of musical self-determination, to which many English musicians give at present a lukewarm allegiance.   If a nation has not faith in its own music, it cannot complain if others have been slow to recognise it ; and faith in English music, as an article of the Englishman's creed, is not as widely held as it should be.   Here again we may learn from France.   The French musician of to-day does not ask whether his composers have written better or worse music than the German classics.   He is content to know that they are writing *his* music, music possessing qualities the appreciation of which is natural to him.   He does not enquire whether the songs of Fauré, Duparc, Chausson, Debussy, or Roussel are worthy to supersede those of Schubert, Schumann, Brahms, or Hugo Wolf.   He acclaims them as French songs which accentuate the æsthetic values of French poetry, and leaves the rest to the world-historian of the future, who will probably chuckle with amusement to find that the point was ever in question.   It is this attitude of the most enlightened Frenchmen that has helped the modern French song to its present level of perfection, for the composer, like Adolphe in Pinero's play, does better under a régime of appreciation, even of the few, than under constant comparison with Henri.   When we cease to grumble at our composers because they do not give us songs like those of Brahms or Wolf, it will not be long before they give us a library of English song worthy of English poetry.   The same applies to other spheres of music. The one thing needed is faith, and faith is the unstated text of M. Aubry's book.

EDWIN EVANS.

PREFACE

" FRENCH Music of To-day " is less a book than a collection of closely related papers, including articles which M. G. Jean-Aubry has contributed in the last few years to various French and foreign reviews ; lectures he has given in Belgium, Switzerland, England, and France ; and " studies for portraits of living musicians." It follows that the chapters comprised in this volume do not present a strict sequence. It will, however, be possible to trace in each of them the course pursued for ten years with convinced ardour by M. G. Jean-Aubry, not on behalf of the French musical renascence, which, having set in at least half a century ago, no longer needs to be explained or defended, but in favour of a more recent and more controversial movement in French music.

I will add with regard to that which is " of To-day," that M. G. Jean-Aubry puts forth startling opinions and ingenious theories, amounting almost to dogmas, which I confess I cannot accept without discussion.

In these earnest days, when one thought alone, the war, obsesses us, will not the appearance of a book devoted to music appear disconcerting, or at least inopportune ? Perhaps, on the contrary, the chapter entitled " French and German Music " will be read with applause, for in this chapter, which alone would suffice to justify the publication of the entire volume, M. G. Jean-Aubry proves with irreproachable good faith that, whilst French art has not ceased to progress, to broaden out in splendour, to make itself manifest by works, tendencies, and characteristics of extraordinary variety, German art since the death of Wagner has entered upon a decline which we have been too amiable to notice sooner. Obviously the advantage gained in this sphere is of far minor importance when compared with the vital considerations which dominate the present conflict. May we not, however, derive from it some satisfaction ?

But, on the other hand, shall we have to forget all that French music owes to the contact of the great German classics ? In many parts of this volume M. Jean-Aubry allows an intention to become manifest—I might call it the leading theme of the book—which consists in regarding as really French solely that music which is linked to the tradition of Rameau and the clavecinists of the seventeenth and eighteenth centuries. " The desire of our present-day musicians," says M. G. Jean-Aubry, " is for infinite variety of expression as opposed to the unity of scholastic composition. Their goal is emancipated expression : it is expressive music, the music of impressions. Couperin, Rameau desired naught else." May not this point of view, which at first appears very broad, be, on the contrary, very narrow? I confess that I do not understand in what manner scholastic discipline can restrain expression, or place obstacles in the way of the utterance of impressions, or how emotion fails to find a free outlet from it. Is not everyone free to express his thought, his feeling, by such means as he chooses ? Do not the symphonic works of Saint-Saëns, Franck, D'Indy, or Dukas, which are conceived in a form of German origin, admit the essentially French qualities of taste, clearness, and sense of proportion ? There is no link, I imagine, connecting Victor Hugo with Racine. Like all the romantics, he felt the influence of Goethe, Schiller, and Byron, just as Berlioz felt the influence of Weber. Is he, therefore, not a French poet ?

Elsewhere M. G. Jean-Aubry rises against " an art which proposes to be utilitarian and to serve some other cause than that of freedom in life and that of beauty." Again, on this point it is possible not to be of his opinion. What matters it if Wagner brought philosophical, Franck or D'Indy moral or religious, Bruneau or Charpentier social, preoccupations to bear upon the conception of their works, or whether these preoccupations proceeded from deliberate intention, or unconscious impulse, if the result for us has consisted in grand, strong, and beautiful emotions ?

Saint-Evremond[1] has said, " The love of pleasure and the avoidance of pain are the earliest and most natural impulses discernible in man." Art has thus every right to be voluptuous. One cannot, however, forbid those whose outlook reveals life in a more serious aspect to express it as they see it.

M. G. Jean-Aubry must excuse me if I rebut some

[1] 1616-1703.

of his theories. To discuss them is to recognise their importance. They will not cause me to forget the keen and rich pleasure I have had from this volume, which I am happy to recommend for perusal.

During recent months the question has often been asked : What is our art to become after the war ? Unless I am mistaken, the most important intellectual movement following upon the war of 1870 was realism, both in literature and in the plastic arts. Afterwards, and perhaps as a kind of reaction, there arose a literary and artistic movement which seems to have its principal source in Wagner's " Parsifal " considered in its philosophical, dramatic, and musical aspect. Hence the " Rose Croix," occultism, Pre-Raphaelism, etc., etc., all capable of being brought back to two terms—asceticism and immobility. Again later, in the safety and the continuity of a prosperous peace which, it was believed, would never be broken, many painters, burning with the fever of novelty, invented, in succession to impressionism, intentionism, cubism, etc., whilst some musicians, less daring, attempted to suppress sentiment in their works and substitute sensation, forgetting that sensation is, on the whole, the preliminary condition of sentiment.

Will the terrific storm through which we are passing bring us back to ourselves by restoring our common sense, that is to say, the taste for clear thought, formal purity and sobriety, the disdain for big effects—in one word, all the qualities that can contribute to make French art in its entirety recover

its admirable character and, whether profound or
subtle, remain for all time essentially French?   I
more than believe it : I am sure of it.

GABRIEL FAURÉ.

CONTENTS

CHAPTER		PAGE
	TRANSLATOR'S PREFACE - -	V
	PREFACE BY GABRIEL FAURÉ -	XXV
I.	FRENCH MUSIC AND GERMAN MUSIC - - - -	I
II.	THE FRENCH FOUNDATIONS OF PRESENT-DAY KEYBOARD MUSIC - - - -	17
III.	STUDIES AND PHYSIOGNOMIES -	49
	1. THE FRIENDS OF MUSIC -	51
	2. A WORD ON MASSENET -	57
	3. GABRIEL FAURÉ - -	62
	4. CLAUDE DEBUSSY - -	69
	5. CONCERNING A BOOK ON CLAUDE DEBUSSY - - -	85
	6. CONCERNING A MUSICAL COMEDY : MAURICE RAVEL'S " L'HEURE ESPAGNOLE " -	97
	7. ALBERT ROUSSEL'S " EVOCATIONS " - - -	110

CHAPTER   PAGE

IV.   SKETCHES FOR PORTRAITS   -   115

     1.   EMMANUEL CHABRIER   -   117

     2.   VINCENT D'INDY   -   -   121

     3.   ERNEST CHAUSSON   -   -   127

     4.   HENRI DUPARC   -   -   132

     5.   PAUL DUKAS   -   -   -   137

     6.   ALBERT ROUSSEL   -   -   141

     7.   FLORENT SCHMITT   -   -   145

     8.   MAURICE RAVEL   -   -   148

     9.   DÉODAT DE SÉVERAC -   -   155

    10.   ERIK SATIE   -   -   -   160

V.   MUSIC AND POETRY   -   -   169

     1.   BAUDELAIRE AND MUSIC   -   171

     2.   VERLAINE AND THE MUSICIANS   191

     3.   OPERATIC POETS   -   -   204

VI.   THREE PERFORMERS   -   -   209

     1.   THE PERFORMER   -   -   211

     2.   RICARDO VIÑES   -   -   214

     3.   JANE BATHORI-ENGEL   -   219

     4.   J. JOACHIM NIN   -   -   223

VII.   FRENCH MUSIC IN ENGLAND   -   235

     INDEX OF NAMES   -   -   -   259

I

FRENCH MUSIC AND GERMAN MUSIC

French Music of To-day

FRENCH MUSIC AND GERMAN MUSIC

IN 1905, on the occasion of a musical festival in Alsace-Lorraine, M. Romain Rolland wrote, " French art is silently engaged in taking the place of German art."

A statement of this kind acquires in course of time a special value from the fact that the author of *Jean-Christophe* is one of those most fully informed in regard to the conditions and achievements of European music, and that within the same article he further stated, " I have never concealed my predilection for German music and I still consider Richard Strauss to be the foremost musical personality in Europe."

We have had occasion since the war to read the sincere and regrettable utterances of M. Romain Rolland concerning his German friends. They have merely confirmed what we have long thought as to the German tendencies of his intellect. They cannot, however, detract from the documentary value of such books as *Some Musicians of Former Days* and *Musicians of To-day*, and they can only add importance to the conviction expressed in 1905. It is, moreover, impossible to forget that so far back as 1904, in a booklet published in German under

B 2

the title *Paris as a Musical City*, M. Romain Rolland contributed to the fame of French music one of his most considered appreciations.

Nowadays those who, a few months ago, were the least concerned with the efforts of our young composers have suddenly awakened to the possibility that France may possess a national music. We have seen M. Camille Saint-Saëns, whose age, and the quality of certain of whose works, gave him a natural right to our respect, engage in a violent attack upon Wagner and demand, in the name of French music, the restoration of compositions which have become definitely obsolete.

It will perhaps be opportune to distinguish between those whose discovery of French music dates from the war and those who have been occupied for many years in adding their testimony, or propagating it so far as lay in their power. However well qualified he may be, by his love of Rameau and of the French clavecinists, to speak in the name of musical France of the past, M. Saint-Saëns has infinitely less right to constitute himself the champion of French music of to-day, for he has expressed himself, regarding this, solely in terms of sarcasm on every occasion.

In any case the *Union Sacrée* has nothing to gain from blindness. It has never been a service to France to engage in an unrestricted campaign of invective. To-day it is less so than ever, and to serve France is the sole concern of every one of us.

If, in the region of thought, as on the battlefield, we hold the certainty of victory, shall we compromise our fame by regrettable excesses ? If it is true that in our race survives the Athenian faculty of fair judgment, it is especially now that we must give proof of it.

In this struggle, in which so many material interests are involved, the moral attention of the world is concentrated upon France. For twenty nations, curious or anxious as to the result of the struggle, she represents the very soul of the conflict. Her attitude in the first months of the war restored her prestige, which had been weakened, in all parts of the world, by her own supineness and the strong determination of her enemies. Her attitude at the approach and on the attainment of victory will further define her new prestige, which will be enhanced by Latin and Slav sympathy, based on faith in her intelligence. Utterances filled with bitterness against Wagner have, since the war, earned for France the smile of neutrals. From Spain, Italy, Switzerland, and America, the Press confronts us with it.

The more our adversary proves himself hateful, the more it behoves us to recognise those qualities by which he might have earned esteem if the extent of his iniquities had not compromised and obliterated his virtues.

It is as profitless to-day as it was yesterday to belittle the genius of Richard Wagner. It is childish to invoke the aid of genealogists and justify the taste which one may still retain for Beethoven by sheltering oneself behind his Flemish antecedents. It would be just as easy for a musical scribe from the Rhine to draw attention some day to the German

heredity of César Franck. These are vain subter-
fuges.

Beethoven is a German of the dawn of the nineteenth century, just as Wagner is a German of the
nineteenth century at its height, and as Bach is a
German of the eighteenth. In attempting to belittle
such genius as was theirs we incur nothing but
ridicule. Shall we hate Haydn, Mozart, and Schubert, who were Austrian, and deny to Liszt, because
he was a Hungarian, the honour of having been the
most fertile source of musical progress in the whole
of the nineteenth century ?

It is unworthy of the present to attempt an attack
upon such a past. The grandeur of German music
from Bach to Wagner is a universal truth. But
to-day we are concerned in the present, and, truly,
here we hold a winning hand. That alone affects
us and of that we must be convinced. Rather
than rise against Wagner (now that his influence,
having taught us all that it was advisable to
retain, has lost its effect on the young French
composers), it would have been better to understand, at the time when they appeared, the
fundamental truths contained in certain articles,
apparently full of paradox, wherein some fifteen
years ago Claude Debussy fought against Germanism,
denounced the dangers of Wagnerism, and rehabili-
tated the art of Couperin and of Rameau.

The playful ingenuity of his points of view and
of his critical method earned for the composer of
Pelléas et Mélisande the reward of laughter and
insult. As for his message,—Who cared ? And

when, with an ardent sense of justice, Claude Debussy defended the memory of Rameau against the exaggerated fame of Gluck,—Who was there to take him seriously ? Was the invasion of the German army really necessary to drive home the truth of the following, which is dated February 7, 1903 :

" We possessed, however, a purely French tradition in the works of Rameau, full of delicate and charming tenderness, of truthful accent, of strict declamation, free from all affectation of profoundness and from the impulse to explain with hammer-blows, to explain breathlessly in a manner which seems to say, ' You are an assembly of very special idiots who understand nothing unless you are previously compelled to accept chalk for cheese.' One is surely permitted to regret that French music has followed, for so long, paths which led it away from this clearness in expression, this precision and conciseness in form, which are the special and significant qualities of French genius."

The revival of some fragments of Rameau's *Castor et Pollux* prompted this justified regret on the part of Claude Debussy, at a time of patient effort, when ingenious temperaments were striving to rediscover the right road and to effect the restoration of French music. Since 1870 two generations have succeeded by their works, by their critical labours, and by their social organisation, in raising French music of to-day to a level higher than it has known for a century, where it is able to challenge comparison with the music of all the ages.

Truly we hold the trump cards against musical

Germany of to-day. Since the death of Richard Wagner, musical Germany drags herself in echoes of Bayreuth, when she is not imitating Brahms, or simply Berlioz.

Richard Strauss himself, despite the power of his symphonic works, the indisputable worth of *Salome* and of *Elektra*, despite his prodigious orchestral skill, Richard Strauss has only the semblance of genius. He personifies in the clearest fashion modern Germany in her essence and in her outward expression. He might be her symbol.

Richard Wagner was the musician of a rising Germany whose industry and patience had lifted her to imperial dignity. Richard Strauss, in spite of all his gifts, or perhaps even because of them, is only the musician of the German decadence, the composer of false power, resting solely upon the strength of the orchestra and upon violent sensation. He represents in reality the best that Germany of to-day can give us. One can measure exactly in his works the disdain of all discrimination in the intellectual factors, the disproportionate multiplication of orchestral units, the strength of material organisation, a self-complacency carried to the most naïve vanity (as in the *Sinfonia Domestica*), and the assurance of bad taste.

Never was this made plainer than when the Russian Ballet troupe gave, two months before the war, the *Legend of Joseph* under the personal direction of Herr Strauss.

Emerging that evening from the opera I expressed to a friend, who has often recalled it since, the clear,

irresistible, and definite sensation I had received of
the decadence of German music.   Like many others,
we had, until then, adopted towards the music of
Richard Strauss an attitude of unprejudiced curiosity, of interest free from disdain.   But then, in
truth, we felt the pretentiousness which would
force the acceptance of anything.   The poverty
of the themes, which reaches the point of vulgarity,
was not even disguised.   Wagnerian imitation was
shamelessly flaunted, enlivened with a sordid Italianism, traces of which can easily be found in the earlier
works of Richard Strauss.   We pass over the silliness
of a libretto which paradoxically aspired to erect
a choregraphic design upon the apotheosis of
chastity, and necessarily achieved nothing but
foolishness.   The mere fact that Strauss had become
a party to such nonsense was in itself significant,
but the music alone, freed from the libretto which
was its foundation, threw a strong light upon the
present situation of German music in the person of
its most notable representative.

The genius of Richard Strauss appeared to us that
day (and we have recorded the impression [1]) an
illusion in which we had once or twice been on the
point of believing, and which now crumbled away
definitely.   Three months later the military genius
of Germany in its turn revealed itself as another
illusion, and German power, great as it might be,
proved itself wanting in precisely those intellectual
virtues which ensure success and justify it in the

[1] *Soliloquy on the Russian Ballets.* (Tribune Musicale,
Brussels, July, 1914.)

eyes of the world. The two phenomena are of the
same class.

In March, 1905, Mr. William Ritter wrote :

" The orchestra of Wagner, of Mahler, of Strauss,
is no longer the agreeable and empirical association
of harmonious instruments employed by Mozart and
Haydn. It is an army in battle array, equipped
with full artillery. Mozart's orchestra might have
been composed of the angelic choir of Cosimo Roselli
and of Gaudenzio Ferrari. Now we have arrived
at lyddite and dum-dum bullets."[1]

Now Mr. William Ritter was one of the most
ardent champions of Strauss and Mahler. His
remark is not the expression of a whim ; it is
essentially a statement of fact.

For the last twenty years the temple of German
music has been no longer at Bonn, or Weimar, or
Munich, or Bayreuth, but at Essen. The modern
German orchestra, with Strauss and Mahler, was
concerned more with the preoccupations of artillery
and the siege train than with those of real music.
It desired to become a rival of Krupp.

The progress of German orchestration was always
directed towards quantity and not towards the
discovery of additional resources in the instruments.
In its most valid manifestations, such as Strauss's
Salome or *Elektra* or Mahler's *Eighth Symphony*,
the effect produced was always startling, disconcerting, or stupefying, rather than the sensation
of a human emotion. It was often impossible at

---

[1] *Studies in Foreign Art.* Introduction. Published by
Mercure de France.

the first hearing of a work by Richard Strauss to resist this overpowering force, but, once the first assault had passed, the mind regained its self-possession and awakened to the emotional inanity and the absence of real musical substance.

It is necessary to have heard, or closely examined, such works. It is impossible to form an exact idea of the music of to-day if one has not done so. But one may say of them, and with stronger reasons, what Claude Debussy said in 1903 of Wagner : " Ought we not long ago to have become acquainted with the whole of the Tetralogy ? In the first place we should have been rid of it, and the pilgrims from Bayreuth would no longer irritate us with their tales."

The pilgrims from Munich, Berlin, and Vienna formerly flooded us with their marvellous stories of the productions of Strauss and Mahler. We have since learned what they amounted to.

In the vast musical agitation which has been seething from one end of Europe to the other for the past forty years, what does the original contribution of Germany amount to, if we compare it to the new impressions, the wealth of originality, the substantial provision for our musical enjoyment that have been and are being furnished by the Russian and French schools, by the Scandinavians from Grieg to Sibelius, by the Spaniards from Albeniz to Turina, Granados and Falla, and by the young Hungarian School with Bartok and Kodaly ?

The music of Europe would not be put back a single step if one were to suppress the output of Strauss or Mahler. It is easy to feel what would be missing in our musical vocabulary had there been no Rimsky, or Albeniz, or Debussy.

Spain, Hungary, England, and Italy furnish proofs to-day of musical effort rooted in their national inspiration, but called forth by the achievements of French composers. New Russia possesses in Stravinsky an admirable and prodigious musician, but France of to-day, from Saint-Saëns and Gabriel Fauré to Maurice Ravel, has produced the chamber music that is richest in emotional, picturesque, and lasting qualities, as well as the symphonic music best qualified to take up, with all the resources of French feeling and intelligence, the legacy of German classical genius in the kingdom of sound.

Even in our own country there has been an irritating tendency to maintain on every occasion that French music lent itself only to minute designs. Obsessed by German conceptions, certain minds were disposed to mistake for pettiness the dimensions of French works, and for power the violence of those hailing from Germany of to-day. Has the war awakened them from their dream?

Shall we make up our minds to realise at last the true greatness and universal value of a period which has seen the birth of Vincent d'Indy's *Symphonie sur un thème montagnard,* Debussy's *Nocturnes, La Mer* and *Iberia,* Albert Roussel's *Evocations,* Florent Schmitt's *Psalm,* Ravel's *Daphnis et Chloe,* Roger-Ducasse's *Suite Française,* and the appearance, in the theatrical sphere, of *Pelléas et Méli-sande*, *Ariane et Barbe Bleue* and *Pénélope* ?

Never has France known a period more richly endowed or more full of new promise. There are still too many people even in our own country—perhaps especially in our own country—who are not yet aware of this. We have become too accustomed to judge the musician or the musical output of the time by the stir they make in the newspapers and in the theatrical world.

The lack of understanding of our musical past has contributed to this lack of perception of the present. Some have believed that if such minds as those of Saint-Saëns, d'Indy, Debussy, or Dukas were interested in French composers of the sixteenth, seventeenth, and eighteenth centuries, it was merely through antiquarian curiosity, whereas they were seeking and finding there the justification of their tendencies and the confirmation of their French taste.

Was not this clearly brought home to us by the musical productions of the *Théâtre des Arts*, where the happy initiative of M. Jacques Rouché brought together the past, present, and future of musical France, where ballets and fragments of operas by Lully or Rameau came together with new works by Ravel and Roussel, and made us appreciate the same qualities of precision and charm ? That which was accomplished for French music in this little *Théâtre des Arts* surpasses in influence the noisy labour of many State-aided theatres.

The greater public is still too ignorant of these activities. or does not understand their full effect

It is still more preoccupied with *virtuosi* than with music. It crowds to hear a tenor and cares little about the works. But in music, as elsewhere, it is minorities that triumph in the end. It is a minority which has created a public in succession for *Samson and Delilah*, *Gwendoline*, *Pelléas* or *Pénélope*. This minority invigorates itself from day to day with new ardour, surrounds young composers with an atmosphere of fervour, and inspires them with an unceasing desire to renew their efforts, to seek with increased passion the precise and lasting expression of our true characteristics.

However fertile and rich French music of to-day may be, and however assured of the direction of her development, it is no more desirable to-day than yesterday, and perhaps even less, that it should be enclosed within a Chinese wall. French art has never benefited by facing inwards. The French mind is rich enough not to fear outside influences, but to assimilate them.

In a recent article,[1] Alfred Casella rightly sets before young Italian musicians anxious for their national art the example of Igor Stravinsky, who studied towards 1908 the works of Debussy, Paül Dukas, and Ravel, with loving care, just as about 1890 Claude Debussy had initiated himself in the beauties of *Boris Godunoff*. Just as the latter gave proof of his essentially French art in *Pelléas et Mélisande*, the former brought new life into Russian art with *Petroushka*, and *The Rite of Spring*.

[1] *Igor Stravinsky and his Art.* (La Riforma Musicale, Turin, March 7, 1915).

The victory of French arms will fill us with a just pride and endow us with a new prestige in the world. It is more than ever our duty to understand what is being accomplished at home and elsewhere. It is more worthy and profitable to penetrate the spirit of the beautiful creations of French music, and assist in making them known beyond the limits of France, than to attack the memory of the immortals whose part in bringing the art into being has been played to its conclusion.

The musical victory of Modern France over Modern Germany is a reality from which we have not yet derived the full benefit. Our own energy must be applied to it, and this can only be achieved in full strength by maintaining, side by side with respect for the great musical past of Germany, the open mind and the lively interest which will be necessary in the greater France of to-morrow.

The task is both noble and pleasant. Moreover, it is facilitated by the abundance and variety of present-day French music.

In their delicate and subtle diversity these composers, sons of a period of deep and powerful sentiments, reflecting a time of misgivings that have reached the certainty of conflict, lovers of mystery and obsessed by clearness, witnesses of a feverish movement alike of ardour and of irony, had unveiled to us the harmonious, smiling yet grave, features of a race whose greatness it has needed this blood-steeped experience to reveal in its fulness. They affirmed the grounds of our belief in the lasting existence of French music.

At their side others, who are younger, gaze open-eyed on the wide spaces of the world, strengthening our joy in the present and preparing to justify our most confident hopes for the future.

From a course pursued for nearly ten years [1] on behalf of French music, these few papers are collected here in order that they may serve, once again, a cause which deserves and attracts deep affections.

The works which furnish the themes of this book have often been my brilliant companions. I have not wished to disguise the warm regard I still retain for them. They teach the joy of life and the thousand qualities of the heart. They are the clear mirror in which are reflected the ardent and delicate features of the French race.

However imperfect this book may be, however incomplete it may be rendered by the extent of the subject itself, which it covers only in some of its aspects, at least it may perhaps derive value from the great love of music to which it owes its conception.

Music is the Ariadne, sad, or smiling, and passionate, who explores by means of her harmonious thread the labyrinth of souls. All I did was to follow her with confident and attentive footsteps.

Sometimes she turned her face towards me ; then I saw that it was sweet, moving, and imbued with the charm of France, which words are powerless to express.

[1] All the chapters of this book, except this one, have appeared in the form of articles or lectures from 1906 to 1914 in France, Switzerland, Hungary, Belgium, or England.

II

THE FRENCH FOUNDATIONS
OF PRESENT-DAY KEYBOARD MUSIC

THE FRENCH FOUNDATIONS OF PRESENT
DAY KEYBOARD MUSIC

THOSE who devote themselves with sympathetic
affection to the study of the manifold forms of art
cannot fail to be overtaken by a feeling that is at
once powerful, moving, and tender. There is no
sentiment more full of sadness, nor at the same time
more consoling. It is the consciousness of their
enduring quality.

We live, time passes, our affection seizes upon a
thousand objects, anxiously chosen, and we imper-
ceptibly come to believe that these objects belong
to us, that none other has known them as we know
them, and that none before us was troubled by the
thoughts that move us. But there comes a moment
when our glance, falling upon a more distant time,
reveals to us a resemblance in the past and a thousand sympathies in common. At first we experience
a certain impatience. It does not please us to think
that we have invented nothing and that we have
merely rekindled ashes that were aglow but neglected. Then these links that bind us to the past
acquire in our eyes great charm, since, if the objects
of our affection are not born solely of ourselves,
at least we are not without claims upon this mysterious past.

Thus is art! The art of our period is not solely

of our day, even when that day happens to see the
opening of its sweetest blooms.   If one is ignorant
of the past one cannot love the present.   We ought
constantly to repeat to ourselves the saying, so
full of truth, of Auguste Comte : " The dead govern
the living."   We all bear within ourselves an infinity
of memories and the deep traces of an often unsuspected past.   In the kingdom of the soul, which is
the widest of all kingdoms, there is but little distance
between the living and the dead.   The accents
of one whom we have loved still govern our speech,
and we often appear to ourselves as only memories
revived.

For the heart, distance is nothing and time
shrinks.   The succession of day upon day is easily
unsettled by the peaceful effort of affection.   Sometimes we think we forget, and are thrown into some
excitement by the incidents of life, but the being
whom we had believed to have passed away for all
time suddenly lives again and reveals to us a marvellous persistence.

Thus is art when one loves it not only for its
fugitive pleasures and its passing semblances, but
when one loves it with all the strength of one's life,
of one's joy, of one's heart.   That which speaks in
the depths of the heart does not pass away.   Art
is not ancient or modern for those who are not
archæologists, but possess living minds, and many
a work written yesterday falls to ruin before the
eternal freshness of poems spoken two thousand
years ago.

It is from this eternal freshness that we must draw

rejuvenated power. It is there that we must seek
the secret of the mysterious words. It is thence
that flashes forth, irresistible and often unperceived,
the flame which animates the movements of our
thought.

Of this truth, those are the best aware who endeavour to be alive, and who love their day for the
words it can as yet scarcely lisp, but in which there
transpires already the desire to widen the human
horizon or to travel beyond it.

And whilst others surround with reverence a past
that is peopled with sumptuously clad corpses, some
there are who succeed so far in unravelling the
sources of fruitful sap in their day that, at their call,
the dead come to life again, and impart to them, with
tenderness or with power, their immortal confidences.

Of this no proof is stronger or more subtle than
that offered by present-day music, and the links
which unite it to a past whose value we misjudge.

Thus it happens that those who are obsessed with
modernity are regarded as lacking fervour for these
mirrors of the past wherein our emotions are reflected, whereas it would be more surprising were
there musical minds that hesitated to recognise
tradition in works on which its character is so incon-
testably impressed.

Tradition, that is the word with which one opposes
all innovation. With it, as has been ably shown by
Mme. Wanda Landowska,[1] one falsifies the expression of older works, whereas it is in the name of

---

[1] Wanda Landowska : *Musique Ancienne*, p. 130. (Published
by *Mercure de France*.)

tradition that, with a little more attentiveness, one justifies the quality of works that endure.

It is thus possible to borrow the utterance of the most pronounced reactionaries by asserting with all sincerity: " One does not evade tradition.   Out of its tradition a race accomplishes naught that endures."   In its aggregate of the characteristics deeply inherent to a race, tradition inevitably reveals itself in works in which race is expressed with the conscious ingenuousness of sincere art.

In the course of centuries foreign additions may accrue to the racial inheritance, but if the race be strong these foreign elements are absorbed, take a new shape, and reveal more than ever the particular quality of the national tradition.

At times the race appears to become languid, and it accepts foreign modes of expression in excessive measure; but in a race like our own such periods are fruitful in reflection, and do not last.

Then an entire people becomes active and its activity makes short work of restoring the links with its tradition, for the art-forms necessarily renew themselves, but the essential forms of a race are not effaced.

It is by its traditional quality that a work of art lives.   To link up tradition it is necessary to go to the very roots of the thought and feeling of a people.

There are, in truth, two kinds of tradition: apparent and real ; lying and truthful ; superficial and deep ; one which one thinks to see, and one which truly exists.

For all French minds desiring beauty, for every

sensitive soul that is captivated by French beauty,
the present age represents a longed-for movement
in musical history : the return to the French tradition. We are recovering ourselves by degrees,
liberating ourselves from more than a century of
foreign influences ; and we are returning by distant
paths to the respect and the love of our true ancestors, whom we have too long held in disdainful
ignorance.[1]

There is at present in France a school of music—
if one may give the name of school to the presence
of certain curious and original minds linked by
similar tendencies ; there is a grouping which begins
to disturb the musical conscience and confront it
with salutary reflections.

The name of Claude Debussy is, in a certain sense,
the binding element of this school, that is free from
the didactic spirit. The works of Debussy are its
strongest, most penetrating, and most considered
expression. Beyond these works there are those
of Sévérac, Ravel, Roussel, Schmitt, and others.

There are still some who, on hearing these works,
assert : " It is interesting, but it is not music,"
a sibylline phrase that would be difficult to explain
if a little examination did not reveal its sense to be :
" It is not music such as we are accustomed to."

And some are to be met with who charge the art

[1] Let it be observed that all this, written in 1908, is only one
statement among many asserting this renewed consciousness of
French tradition that, a few years before the war, seized upon
all forms of thought and of art. This renascence of the French
idea was perhaps not without effect upon the national unanimity
that was a matter of surprise to the foreigner, and for France
herself, in August, 1914.

of Debussy and his colleagues with not being French art. Strange irony of terms ! Have most of those who advance such opinions endeavoured to unravel the roots and characteristics of French art ? Have they explained to themselves the nature of the French musical tradition in whose name they speak ? And are they aware that the works which are their models are not associated with their race ?

Meanwhile there are works of charm, feeling, often deep whilst charming, which prove that we have had in France a period of admirable musicians who were deeply and delightfully French.

During more than a century these musicians have been forgotten. Those who knew them despised them, believing them to be superficial and negligible minds, remote from the taste of the day. If they were remote from that taste it was for an excellent reason : they were delicately and really French, and for more than a century there had been no French music in France

This abandoning of our music may be dated about 1770. In Bussely's work on *The Present Conditions of Music in France and Italy*, published in 1771, one may note his remark concerning Mlle. Diderot, whom he states to be one of the best clavecinists in Paris, and possessed of an extraordinary knowledge of modulation, adding, however : " Although I had the pleasure of hearing her for some hours, she did not play a single French piece. All was Italian or German."

Yet the epoch of the great clavecinists had scarcely closed. Towards 1770 the Italianism, which Lully had deformed a century before, and whose elements Couperin and Rameau had transformed according to the principles of French genius, reasserted itself, thanks to the complicity of *virtuosi*. The signs of it that may be discerned in the works of Royer or Duphly only needed to spread, and were easily to reach the opera with the assistance of *opéra-comique*.

At the same time, as M. Claude Debussy has so wittily said : " Marie-Antoinette, who never ceased to be an Austrian until that sentiment was taken from her, once and for all, imposed Gluck upon French taste. Since that blow our fine traditions have become falsified and our need of clarity submerged." [1]

Agitated, confused, shaken to her roots by the revolution and its consequences, France could not at the time concern herself with considered art-work

Italian and German influences continued to have concurrent effect, the theatre possessing special attraction ; and, little by little, one saw come into being that hermaphroditic product, that strange mixture, described, no doubt by antiphrasis, as French opera : the creation of an Italian, Rossini ; and a German, Meyerbeer.

We are not here concerned with disputing the value of *Orpheus*, or of the *Barber of Seville*, or even of *Les Huguenots* ; but is it in the name of Gluck, Rossini, and Meyerbeer, three foreigners, that one is entitled to defend the French tradition ? Would it not be possible to quote three names of French,

[1] Claude Debussy : *Concerning " Hippolyte et Aricie."* (*Le Figaro*, March 7, 1908.)

truly French musicians, representing a powerful factor between 1770 and 1830 ? Except out of curiosity, who still cares for the works of Lesueur ? Is it Auber's *Fra Diavolo* that will stand for a date in musical history ?

French tradition, where art thou ?

Years pass. Beethoven, Schubert, Schumann, Weber, penetrate gradually. Liszt, that great and admirable propagandist, confronts the musical races one with another, sets the new ideas in motion and stirs them, and then it is Wagner whose authoritative and violent genius imposes his tendency on French music. Reyer submits to it, Vincent d'Indy propagates it, even to Massenet, all experience it.

French tradition, where art thou ?

What musicians are there before 1880 to represent French tradition, with dignity and some standing, in the eyes of the unbiassed musical historian ? Berlioz and Saint-Saëns ; for the Italianism of Gounod, even when he is Wagnerian, does not equitably represent our race.

The case of Berlioz would suffice to throw light upon the spontaneity of tradition. The case is unique, an example of a prodigious gift that, starting from a daring ignorance, attained to a singular expressiveness ; this Berlioz who began his acquaintance with Bach only when at the Villa Medici, and who can have studied only scraps of Beethoven at a time when the eight scenes of *Faust* and a large portion of the *Fantastic Symphony* were already written.

And that is the man who first restored some of

the links of the French tradition, because his ignorance of foreign influences permitted him to recover in his own personality the expressive qualities of his race.

There are in Berlioz many unsound elements. His work bears the trace of the grandiloquence of his times. But there is in *Les Troyens,* and in the duets of *Romeo and Juliet,* an earnest and tender beauty, smiling or sad, expressive without stress : a truly French beauty.

Yet Berlioz seems to have had no influence except in Germany, where to-day Richard Strauss, having transformed it by the leaven of his own gifts and talent, represents its accomplishment. Saint-Saëns, on the contrary, astonishingly intelligent, qualified to understand all, treating with the same felicity all styles in music, ought to have been the leader of a school, if his too inquisitive mind had been able to form a definite resolution of the kind which stamps a genius.

One may reproach him with his " try-all " tastes, his often excessive skill, his diverse and changeable curiosities. But in his taste for clarity, even in his curiosity, in his witty and sensitive manner, there are some of the greater qualities of the French tradition, still mingled, alas, with all the influences, too often apparent, of Beethoven, Schumann, Liszt, or Wagner.[1]

Since then we have had César Franck proposed to us as a French master.

[1] It is well known that, since then, Saint-Saëns has denied his indebtedness to the last-named.

It is impossible to be lacking in reverence for the man of genius who composed the *Beatitudes*. But is it French, this mysticism, this ignorance of irony, this taste for metaphysic, this readiness to take everything seriously, this need to prove something, this absence of critical sense, this imperviousness to the strong sensuousness of the Latins, and this taste in formal development in which can be found the characteristics of the Teutonic race?

Apart from these, what musicians are there to defend, in our eyes, the French tradition? Bizet, whose recently published correspondence places him in a not very favourable light, and whose works have importance only in themselves, allowing neither principle nor example to be deduced from them? Lalo, who is neglected, and who really represents the pretty, delicate, charming aspect of our musical intellect? Chabrier, who is unappreciated, and who embodies its robust, witty, ironic aspect? But these have as yet had no influence upon the musical public.

What is then the tradition in whose name those speak who find that modern music is not French? When one traces their origin, one recognises that their French tradition in music is that of Beethoven, Mendelssohn, or Schumann, when it is not that of Rossini, or Wagner.

In France we have all acquired our musical education almost exclusively from the German classics. That is certainly of more worth than the sole teaching of the *virtuosi* of the piano. But at the present day we are concerned with something else. We are

confronted with efforts made to ensure to France her
own mode of musical expression, and here is the
public scarcely beginning to understand that there
have been times when we were familiar with forms
of music and with compositions in which the particular characteristics of our genius were reflected.

There are a few of us whom the love of our modern
musicians has led towards our admirable men of
the Renaissance, towards those clavecinists of the
seventeenth and eighteenth centuries.   The oblivion
of our true traditions is signalised by the harmful
neglect of these masters, and the regard for our
traditions, by the return towards their eternal
freshness and their beauty of substance.

Yes, sometimes, in the course of our musical studies,
our attention was drawn to a piece by Couperin
or Rameau, just as one claims to describe our
admirable poetic efflorescence of the sixteenth
century with the aid of a sonnet by Joachim du
Bellay, a rondeau by Rémy Belleau, followed by some
poems of Ronsard.   Until fifteen or twenty years
ago, apart from a few monomaniacs, there were
none to interest themselves in Rameau, Couperin,
Dandrieu, and others.

Somewhat suddenly there was a revival of curiosity concerning them.   By whom was it revived,
or rather whose names do we find at the head of this
movement of reparation ?   Precisely those which
mark the summits of present-day music in France :
Saint-Saëns, one of the founders of the *Société
Nationale de Musique* (which for forty years has
witnessed the flowering of all French music) and

at the same time director of the complete edition of Rameau's works, that important monument of reparation of the twentieth century to the eighteenth century in music. And with Saint-Saëns, whom do we find associated in the achievement of this edition? The organist Guilmant, and the three names most representative of this French day: Vincent d'Indy, Paul Dukas, and Claude Debussy.

Is not the coincidence truly singular? There is no chance in this. In art there is only the logic of consciences, of wills and of facts. Vincent d'Indy who, together with Charles Bordes, founded the *Schola* to co-ordinate the efforts which aimed at restoring our music from the thirteenth to the eighteenth centuries, presides to-day over the *Société Nationale de Musique*, and conducted the other day the rehearsals of Rameau's *Hippolyte et Aricie* and *Dardanus*. Paul Dukas composed his celebrated Variations on a theme by Rameau. Finally, Claude Debussy has written an admirable piece, full of noble gravity, entitled *Hommage à Rameau*, and is it not also the composer of *Pelléas et Mélisande* who wrote some time ago:

" Why should we not regret this charming manner of writing music that we have lost, just as it is impossible to discover the traces of Couperin? It avoided all redundance and was possessed of humour. We scarcely dare nowadays to own a sense of humour for fear of being lacking in grandeur, to which we breathlessly aspire without attaining to it very often." [1]

[1] Claude Debussy, *l. c.*

No, all this is not due to chance. Those minds are alert. They have appeared at a time when French music has begun to feel the need of emancipation, of being true to itself, of liberating itself from Germanism, whether hailing from Beethoven or from Wagner.

Let none repeat that music is a universal art, independent of nationalities and races : Genius can attain to some degree of universality when it bears the name of Shakespeare or Beethoven, but even those are, none the less, the one an Englishman of the sixteenth century, and the other a German of the end of the eighteenth. All the more does an aggregate of works bear the stamp of its period and its nationality, especially in the world of music, an art of the senses, an art more closely linked than any other with those differences of mood, those movements of character which stamp the variety of races.

It would be well in future to examine our modern compositions, more logically than has been done in our generation, in the light of a perfect knowledge of our sixteenth, seventeenth, and eighteenth centuries. One would then discern, better than is possible in the arguments stated here, how the special characteristics of the French mind perpetuate themselves from the seventeenth to the twentieth centuries in spite of a century of foreign influences.

There is certainly no question of comparing the method of composition in French works at the commencement of the eighteenth century and at the commencement of the twentieth. Let us only consider that in the space of these two centuries

there has occurred the most rapid evolution an art
has ever known. It is a question of examining
throughout the musical contents, more or less
complex, of these works, the spirit that governed
its inflections. It would be equally possible to
examine it in vocal or dramatic compositions, but
perhaps it will reveal itself more fully in the music
of the keyboard.

The fashions and cults of yesterday do not constitute tradition. To discover it, it is necessary
to penetrate further into, and even beyond, an art,
towards the springs at which its sap is refreshed and
renewed.

The features of our music are those of our mind
and our temperament. To determine these features is not easy, but to know them it suffices to
have had passionate enjoyment from our works
of art.

Clearness first. Not the external clearness of
works which are devoid of thought, like some
Italian compositions, but the clearness of the mind
that has reflected, and that puts forth in good order
the fruits of its meditation.

In order, clearness ; and in expression, precisely
that quality which has been described as the fear
of emphasis. This we find as much in *Dardanus* as
in *Pelléas*, in *Thésée* as in *Ariane et Barbe Bleue*.
We find the opposite in *Manfred*, and in *Tristan and
Isolde*, in association with other qualities which are
not ours.

It is not that we do not know how to be lyrical,
but with us irony is ever on guard. We are too

enamoured of proportion to yield for long to the intention, as the saying is, of taking the moon in our teeth.

. The avoidance of all that is redundant ; knowledge without the desire to display it ; a horror of pedantry ; a taste for pleasantry and for wit ; these are features that may be found revealed as clearly and as constantly in the pieces of Couperin, Dandrieu, or Daquin as in those of Ravel, Roussel, or Sévérac.

The desire, definite or vague, of our present-day musicians, is to reject all the philosophical, metaphysical, or literary theories with which the greatest German geniuses have stuffed their music. Assuredly our music, like our intellect, lacks certain qualities which are sometimes abundant in the Teutonic and Slav races ; but a better knowledge of its origins can only lead to increased consciousness of itself and of its powers.

The desire of our present-day musicians is an infinite variety of expression as opposed to a unity of scholastic composition. Their goal is emancipated expression : expressive music, the music of impressions. Couperin, Rameau, neither wished nor accomplished more.

It is the French mind in music that is here under discussion. One must see in this matter neither chauvinism nor national vanity. It is solely a question of determining our mind with precision.

For centuries we have borne within our temperaments the subtle sense of atmosphere, the love of delicate vibrations. We have a soul that is at once

D

sensitive and ironic, as far removed from puritanism as it is from grossness, a soul impregnated with the sensuous pantheism which is the eternal strength of our genius. We possess the Mediterranean taste for rhythm, and here we find reviving in our most modern composers, with an entirely musical dignity, the cult of dances, harmoniously projected by the formal sense, and the cult of ironic wit, harmoniously projected by the intellect. And all this is steeped in a feeling for the picturesque in which Debussy, Ravel, Sévérac and the others reveal an ingenuity, and impressions which rival those of our clave-cinists, whose evocations are not tarnished by the dust of more than a century and a half.

A glance merely at the titles of the compositions will convince one of this love of the picturesque and of evocation. We find in them not closely defined programmes but themes of evocation. When to-day Claude Debussy entitles a piece *Poissons d'Or*, he has not the pretension to depict. Ichthyology does not fall within the province of music. But he desires to evoke the impression of something glittering and fugitive plunged in a fluid atmosphere —something that is gone in a flash and that quickly renews its rapid movement in diverse directions with the colour-play of all that gambols in the sunshine.

If one listened to music a little more with the ears, with feeling, not sentimentality, but with intellectual sensuousness, this question would not need discussion.

By their regard for the picturesque as by the characteristic features of the French intellect, which are plainly discernible in both, the music of the past and that of to-day reveal themselves as much nearer to each other than one might at first believe.

In one, as in the other, we are concerned with a music of the senses in which the regard for expression predominates over formal considerations. It is programme music in which is revealed the taste for rhythms and for picturesque sonorities, and which is thus led to the selection of subjects which are similar or proximate. But a French musical tradition could not be based upon a mere resemblance of titles, were these not narrowly associated by the spirit which animates these appeals to the imagination.

The twentieth century will witness the musical awakening of many nations who ranked among the greatest in the past, and have seemed to lose their vigorously national features. Already Spain on the one hand, and England on the other, are endeavouring to bring about the rebirth of a genuinely national efflorescence by the study of their true musical ancestry, and of their wealth of folktune, and they remember now having given birth, the one to Cabezón and Victoria, the other to Byrd and Purcell. The spirit of renewal has spread even to Italy, which, perhaps, may see again splendours to be compared with those of Monteverde.

France has embarked upon her musical emancipation. It is not yet assuredly accomplished. As yet it is only the dawn, but the dawn is gracious and moving, and it is precisely for that reason that, to-day more than ever, we must remember that French music does not date from yesterday, that it possesses many charming, tender, and witty pages, and that a clavecin two hundred years ago has often sufficed to evoke sentiments whose truth and freshness, recalled by these pages, still come to life for us with a mysterious and delicate power.

French clavecin music does not commence with Couperin, but fifty years earlier with Jacques Champion, known as de Chambonnières. It would be wrong to neglect this charming spirit. It is he who must be considered as the starting-point of the French school, and, if he was neither its most complete nor its most powerful manifestation, at least he remains one of the most delicate and most seductive.

Chambonnières was the first in France to succeed deliberately in emancipating the music of the clavier from that of the organ. If it is true that Frescobaldi had already attempted it in Italy, the earnestness of that admirable musician drew him too strongly towards religious forms of expression to permit him to liberate himself.

In the works of Chambonnières one can remark that charming frankness which is a feature of his whole century. He introduces at the clavecin the dance-forms, especially those which were beginning to be abandoned and in which, being no longer concerned with the dancer, the musician is free to infuse infinite variety and fancy. In his slow movements one often discerns a tender feeling, which is the first attempt towards the delicate psychology

and the discreet tenderness which were to be revealed later by Couperin, Rameau, and Dandrieu.

Chambonnières was, moreover, an admirable
performer on the clavecin, celebrated for his light
touch, and the incomparable rapidity of his fingering.[1]
The principal clavecinists of the period, whose works
have been handed down to us, were his pupils ;
among others, d'Anglebert, Le Bègue, and the three
Couperins.

Of the numerous family of the Couperins, which,
during two centuries, gave musicians to France,
whether composers or performers, François has
deservedly remained the most celebrated ; and was
it not with justice that he was named " Couperin
the Great " ?

Though the dates place him in the reign of Louis
XIV, Couperin the Great has not quite the spirit
of the *Grand Siècle*. A true Parisian of Paris,
inclined to raillery and humour, jesting and irony,
yet fastidious and full of feeling, he calls to our
minds much more a certain air of the period of the
Précieuses, and at the same time some features of
the reign of Louis XV.

He is a unique figure in our ancestry. We shall
not meet again with that airy grace. Others will
appear with more melancholy, deeper expression,
or more emotional intensity, but we shall not see
again such penetrating charm, such knowledge of
the art of pleasing, the ingenuous skill of a smiling
nature. Let none be misled. His art is not only

[1] *Cf.* Père Mersenne: *Universal Harmony* (1636); and Le
Gallois : *Letter to Mlle. Reygnaut de Sallier* (1680).

on the surface, and there are witnesses to record for us that, in his own day, Couperin was considered a profound composer.[1]

We are nowadays too accustomed to see depth only in weighty treatises, and in intellects that are somewhat heavy. Throughout the works of Couperin there is present a fastidious revelation of intelligent psychology, with evidence of an ingenious power of observation, and of a satisfaction in living and feeling that is fairly common among Frenchmen.

Moreover, life in those days was less arduous for musicians than it is apt to be at present.

In those days, musicians were petted. Many great nobles considered themselves in honour bound to maintain a small orchestra in their suite, and there was rivalry between great houses. Some of them even engaged servants only on the condition that they were musical.

There raged among the highest classes a veritable fever for music. Constantly associated with the diversions of society, music was scarcely commencing to part company with the dance, and was at first limited to gathering up the forms shed by the latter : *Allemande, Courante, Sarabande, Galliarde.* For some time yet we shall see persist the *Gavotte, Passepied,* and *Gigue.* Allemande, Courante, and Sarabande will constitute the elements of the suite which Bach and Handel will raise to a dignity from which proceeds the entire æsthetic of the musical forms of the nineteenth century.

As has been discerningly said by M. Jules Ecorche-

[1] Abbé de Fontenay: *Dictionary of Artists.* (Paris, 1776.)

ville : " Music was not then the Tristanesque art which tears us from the world, but, on the contrary, a manifest sign of worldly preoccupations, and a manner of adorning and enlivening the pleasures of society."[1]

What charming discourses these clavecin pieces hold forth to us ! How fragrant are their titles and their subjects with elegance and wit, and with the amiable and fastidious spirit that can speak of all things without fuss.

And do we not cut a somewhat sorry figure in neglecting music which gave pleasure to great men, Bach among others ?

It goes without saying that Bach took a deep interest in the French performance of these works, for the French instrumental executants had already given proof in their performance of the native elegance that still qualifies many of our modern interpreters. But Bach took an even greater interest in the musical substance of French compositions for organ and clavecin. He investigates their melodic quality. He borrows themes from French masters, notably from Couperin.

That does not prevent Voltaire, who was often more accurately informed, from writing : " In the century of Louis XIV, music was still in the cradle. A few languishing songs ; a few tunes, mostly composed in Spain, for violin, guitar, and the theorbo, were all that was known."[2]

[1] Jules Écorcheville : *Twenty Orchestral Suites of the Seventeenth Century in France.*

[2] Voltaire : *The Century of Louis XIV.*

We will not say, as Mme. de Sévigné said of Lully,
" I do not believe that there exists any other music
under heaven," but it really is delicate and durable
music.

This musical literature is at present, more than
ever, an educational necessity. Amédée Méreaux
himself wrote in *The Clavecinists :* " This musical
literature was, a few years ago, still regarded as a
curiosity.   In our day it has acquired usefulness.   It
has become an indispensable element of education." [1]

Its necessity has not yet been sufficiently realised
by the majority.   There are still too many who refuse
to see in it more than a curiosity for archæologists ;
who are unaware that in all these works there is a
grace and an expression of feeling that are not
behind those of our day.

The works of Couperin are copious and varied.
Four volumes of exquisite pieces cannot reveal
their quality merely in a few familiar numbers.
There are too many that remain unknown : *Le
Bavolet flottant* ; *Les Musettes ;* the *Badine* in which
runs a mincing affectation, a portrait which we
cannot recall without the smile that is awakened
in the heart of the fastidious by the elegance, the
wit, and the thousand piquant and elusive tricks of
feminine coquetry ; the purity of the *Lys naissants* ;
the delightful and ingenious variety of *The Dominos*,
variegated to the most delicate and mysterious
Domino couleur d'invisible ; and the *Bergeries* ;
and so many more pieces in which the feeling for
nature, which had almost completely vanished from

[1] Amédée Méreaux : *The Clavecinists*, p. 1.

literature, appears with a healthy and attractive freshness, amid which the cult of the dance-forms finds a favourable setting ; and *Le Rossignol en amour*, in which is found one of the most graceful themes fashioned by Couperin, that king of grace ; and the *Carillon de Cythere*, which does not sound the departure, the " embarking " of which Watteau was to evoke the unconstraint tinged with sadness, together with the reticences of a soul that seems already to doubt the lasting of love,—it sounds the charm of the exquisite hour under the softness of skies indulgent to harmonious tenderness ; the witty exaggeration of the *Fastes de la Grande et Ancienne Ménestrandise* ; the *Arlequin* for which Couperin wrote the direction : *grotesquement ;* and ever so many more pieces.

Fastidious, enchanting, observant, witty, mocking, slily malicious, ironic, biting, the clavecin assumes with Couperin every variety of accent in turn.

Freshness needs to have a rare quality if it is not to be tarnished after two centuries. Works claimed to be more profound will have passed away while these will still have life, echoing the soul of François Couperin, immortal and smiling figure of immortal French grace.

The distance from Couperin to Rameau is not only that between two somewhat remarkable personalities, or between two differently constituted societies, but it also includes all that divides, one from another, two great periods of musical history ; and the very characters of these two men display at once the divergencies and the respective tendencies of these periods, without thereby ceasing to remain, by the features they possess in common, two essentially French figures.

Couperin is the sum of amiable Parisian grace, the sum of the sociable spirit, the love of dancing, of company, of elegant suppers, of amusement, of bonds in which love is less important than pleasure and than the delight one finds in turning gallant phrases in their honour.

Rameau is the French spirit of reason awakening. He is the solitude that reflects, the patience that learns. His is the enquiring spirit of the *Encyclopédie* : the circumspect intelligence applying itself to the study of the human heart and of the means of expression at its disposal.

Couperin is the musician as he appears to Guez de Balzac, to Voiture, to Saint-Evremond. Rameau is the equal and the colleague of Voltaire, Diderot, and d'Alembert ; and in more than one instance his effort precedes theirs in the same direction.

We are enabled to inform ourselves of the evolution of the musical spirit in French society of the seventeenth and eighteenth centuries by the agreeably written volume of M. Jules Écorcheville entitled *From Lully to Rameau,* in which this remarkable evolution, and the conflicts to which it gave rise, are studied in detail.

An absorbing concern with music then makes itself felt in the smallest writings, even those which seem by their nature the furthest removed from such questions.

After the obsession with music came the time for

reflection upon the subject. An attempt was made to confine the obsession within the limits of reason and of definitions.

Unable to accomplish this, the *Encyclopédistes* had the presumption to reject music with its limitations as a mere art of imitation, amenable to charm but not to reason; and that is how they came to attack the very composer who was doing naught else but apply to music the method and spirit which they brought to science and literature.

A strange and massive figure was Rameau, perhaps the greatest in the whole of French music; for Colossus as Berlioz is, he unfortunately possesses feet of clay that cannot always be concealed.

Rameau embodies the most astonishing balance of science, will-power, and inspiration. Nothing extravagant characterises him. It may be that he is crabbed and savage, because the obsession of the problems on which he aspires to throw light compels him to solitude; but how much the more thoroughly does the most vivid feeling pierce through in a thousand places!

Plasticity of the rhythms, a sense of orderly life, delicacy, and care to maintain the balance of expression, these are the features of Rameau. Do there exist other essential qualities to which our national genius can lay claim with better right, or which are more suitable to define our French tradition, whether it be studied in the sixteenth, the eighteenth, or the twentieth century?

When Rameau died, at the beginning of September, 1764, it was discovered that nothing was known of him, at all events in the period in which he developed ; for the honours and privileges which were heaped upon him during the latter part of his life made of him one of the principal figures of his day. Little by little, the life of Rameau has been unravelled, though not all the desired information is available concerning it. But of greater importance to us are the principal features of the man and his character, and among them his love of solitude, and the slowness and conscientiousness of his development.

Let us especially bear in mind that this man, who raised French opera to a level which even Gluck did not surpass, had not at fifty years of age composed a single opera. With admirable patience and determination he awaited the hour when, confident of his powers, he should be able to carry out his purpose.

Before the age of fifty he had published only his theoretical books and his volume of pieces for the clavecin, but the latter alone would suffice to make his fame secure.

In the eyes of certain minds of his day Rameau passed for a scholar, a pedagogue, and no more : a musician with a curious interest in the bizarre grouping of chords. He is a mathematician, a geometrician who has taken it into his head to write music and naturally succeeds in constructing sonorous patterns in which the proportions are accurate, but soul and ear are disappointed.

Thus thinks Grimm ; and Diderot, in *Le Neveu de Rameau*, writes :

" This musician who delivered us from the plain-song of Lully ; who has written so many unintelligible visions and so many apocalyptic truths on the theory of music . . . and from whose pen we have a certain number of operas in which are harmony, odds and ends of song, disconnected ideas, clashes, thefts triumphs, lances, glories, murmurs, breathless victories, dance tunes that will last for ever, and who, after burying the Florentine, will himself be buried by the Italian *virtuosi*."

Jean Baptiste Rousseau goes so far as to insult him :

> Distillateur d'accords baroques
> Dont tant d'idiots sont férus,
> Chez les Thraces et les Iroques
> Portez vos opéras bourrus.[1]

Have we not recently met with similar invective aimed at Debussy and his admirers ?

Should not such expressions, coming as they do from intelligences that were concerned with music, induce those who are in revolt against new works to-day to proceed with caution ?

Can we believe to-day that it is Rameau, w ɔ is clearness itself, Rameau, harmony and melody personified, of whom such things were said ? Voltaire had shown greater sagacity in saying: " Rameau has made of music a new art."

Yet Rameau, in the care he takes to give his

[1] Free translation—

> Coiner of the strange, weird chords
> Hearts of idiots let them ravage,
> Take your uncouth operas
> To the Hottentot and savage

knowledge a solid foundation, retains the virtues of French logic and the fear of pedantry. Here is what he writes to Houdard de la Mothe :

"You will see forthwith that I am not a novice in art and that I do not appear to draw largely upon my skill in my productions, in which I endeavour to conceal art by art itself."

This admirable phrase is a subtle example displaying the most simple dignity and the intellectual fastidiousness of what is best in French genius.

This man, the most learned in music of his day, declares that his works do not display his skill. That is especially noteworthy.

Ironical, biting, solitary, unattractive to those who did not know him, Rameau obeyed only his artistic conscience, to which he caused the great nobles and even the King to submit. Behind this exterior, and this dignity that readily took umbrage, were the deepest feeling, great tenderness, and the strictest judgment upon himself. Did he not say after his opera *Zoroastre* : "From day to day I improve in taste, but I no longer have genius."

Let us but listen to the *Tendres Plaintes*. Truly, does not the emotional quality of such music equal the feeling of Schumann himself? Though less ardent, the emotion is none the less deep. And to bring in Schumann for comparison is to go almost to the confines of emotion in music. If it pleased us to forget for a moment our involuntary prejudices, if it pleased us to return with a little more assiduity to these exquisite masters who are neglected on the pretext of frivolity, we should soon realise that, in spite of the lapse of two centuries, the spirit and the soul in these works are much nearer to ourselves than all possible Schumanns, however subtle.

But, in the eighteenth century, feeling in music is not only present in examples by Couperin or Rameau. In Daquin, in Royer, and especially in Dandrieu, are to be found other instances ; of the latter, if not the three volumes of clavecin pieces, at least one of selected works, should be republished. If our acquaintance were limited only to the *Tendres Reproches* it would enable us to judge to what degree simplicity can be moving, and how a simple theme on the clavecin can still reach the heart when it is the expression of a harmonious and sensitive soul.

As soon as we have entered upon this inexhaustible garden of French flowers we are overwhelmed with the charm and grace it contains, and with all that still responds to our souls after two centuries.

We soon learn to love music of the seventeenth and eighteenth centuries not as an object of curiosity, but as a living reality, akin to ourselves, more than ever present, which awakens within us the confused and disturbing consciousness of the things that endure.

There we rediscover the sources of our own true genius. We learn to understand by what delightful bonds our modern music is linked to the past, and we discover a thousand pretexts to take up again in the domain of music the affectionate defence of French sensibility.

(1908)

III

STUDIES AND PHYSIOGNOMIES

THE FRIENDS OF MUSIC

(*To Cyprien X. Godebski*)

IN the world, writes Chamfort,[1] we have three kinds
of friends : those who love us, those who do not
trouble about us, and those who hate us.

Like ourselves, music possesses in the world three
kinds of friends. Those who do not trouble about
it are the people who go to concerts to meet their
acquaintances and to arrange for the employment
of their week ; those who applaud *virtuosi*, however
bad the quality of the compositions they perform ;
those who, after dinner, insist on asking for a piece
of music or a song, the opening of which, by some
mischance, always happens to coincide with their
conversation ; those who applaud only in batches,
and if the work performed bears the name of a
composer on whom one may safely depend ; and
those critics who find in music no more than an
opportunity of writing : in a word, those who are
always ready to hear music, and never ready to listen
to it.

The friends who hate music are those who profess
to love it, and appreciate only its dead bones. They
speak volubly of it, and despise those who do not
love it. They constantly embrace music only to

[1] Born 1741 ; died 1794.

E2

stifle it. They dissect it, unaware of their preliminary murder of it, and without understanding that the work they have pulled to pieces lacks only one thing, but that the most important: *life*.

Those people have always a theory in readiness. If a new composition is brought to them it does not take them long to break its limbs, open its body, correct its shape and prove to you that it is not formed in accordance with the rules and principles.

With the friends of this kind, no fancy is possible. They have a mould, press it down on the compositions, and clip away all that protrudes. Their musical life is spent with a magnifying glass, an eraser, and a pair of scissors.

The supreme quality of a work, for them, is to be fashioned according to their rules. Only on that condition is it music. They found schools in which the art of writing a sonata or the manner of treating a symphony is taught in twenty lessons. They know all the recipes, which they have classified in their musical cookery-books. They spend their lives in the kitchen.

They teach how to develop an idea mathematically without giving a moment's attention to its intrinsic quality, believing, as they do, that the sauce will make the fish palatable even when it is not fresh. They expand and discuss, perorate, and place restrictions upon what is music and what is not. Really, Molière would still find plenty to do.

Never, perhaps, has music been infested more than to-day with these friends who hate it. Graduates without taste, journalists without culture, decrepit porers over archives, have intruded themselves into music like rats into a ship. They imagine that they cause it to travel, when it is much more likely that they can only defile or infect it.

For what do they care about feeling, grace, charm, emotion, or all that from first to last goes to make the unrivalled power of music, all that causes music to be not merely the diversion of well-fed stomachs, or a pretext for theories, but the unique confidant of our hours of joy and pain, evoking earthly land-scapes of inner horizons ? What do they care for all that music contains of tenderness, of faith, of voluptuousness, of elevation, or of rapture ? They occupy themselves with the measurement of master-pieces. They accumulate anthropometric records. They possess the art of making everything they touch intolerably boring.

They have thus taken possession of certain masters, and, in the first place, Bach, the supreme genius who assumes every aspect. Of this eighteenth-century man, who possesses the secret of meditating and of smiling, who knows, according to the moment, how to be grave or joyous, how to compel or to charm, they have made an old college prefect, an ill-humoured censor, a musical-box, a metronome : boredom in order, and order in boredom.

Under the rod of these people generations have trembled, and young girls can be met who ought to be all feeling, grace, and joy of living, and who say to you, " Schumann, Mozart, Chopin " in a dis-dainful tone and raise their eyes to heaven with ecstasy in pronouncing the name of Bach. But what a Bach is theirs! Good heavens!

Then one catches oneself wishing to meet and associate with people who have less assurance in the knowledge of the rules, people unable to write a page and capable of confusing the numbers of Beethoven's symphonies, but who love the works with more candour and spontaneity, and who seek to improve their knowledge of them only in order to control their emotion and imbue it with more lasting elements. Such people may sometimes allow themselves to be led astray by a mediocre work, but will never approach a musical composition save to seek in it the satisfaction of the ear or of the heart, and to find what the composer expressed in it, whether joy or sorrow, aspiration or serenity—in one word: *life*.

The friends who love music are not always disposed to listen to that of the most serious purport. They appreciate, according to the moment, immense works, or such as are more minute. They are able to derive, according to the hour, as much satisfaction from a song as from a music-drama. They are no more given to the idolatry of large works than to the predilection for small ones. They do not believe that the word symphony followed by three-quarters of an hour's music necessarily reveals an important work, nor that one need despise two pages of piano music in which refined writing is associated with humour or with feeling.

They sometimes feel tired to exhaustion by what they have most loved. They abandon masters

only the more eagerly to return to them. There
are days on which they are weary of Schumann's
romanticism, of Wagner's æsthetic ideas, of César
Franck's soaring, and they make no attempt to
conceal that they do not feel compelled to worship
every genius, or to heap invective on those who leave
them unmoved.

They conform within a certain measure to the
fundamental tastes inherent to their nature, and
to the sum of all that contributes to form the culture
of a period. They maintain equal distance from
pedants and from snobs. If they have enjoyed
Pelléas, *Boris*, or *The Rite of Spring*, if these works
have given them occasion for experiencing emotion
or pleasure, they have not assumed the conviction
that music had its beginning in these works and that
by them the entire past was cancelled.

They endeavour to be ready to reject nothing that
they have not proved, and to accept nothing on the
strength of its label. They do not profess their
love of music or announce it to all comers as if they
truly did music great honour, and it could not exist
without them.

The true friends of music sometimes appear to
forget it. They know that there is something un-
lovely in the parade of one's affections, and that
there is no love but demands silence if it is to endure.
They do not speak only of music. They do not
slay for its sake. They admit that one may not
love it, and that there is no incomparable merit
in loving it, though it is an infirmity not to be susceptible to it. They do not throw themselves upon

works, like the wolf upon Little Red Riding-Hood.

They apply a better sense of proportion ; their ecstasies are intimate, and their joys are deep enough not to require so many incoherent words. They find a thousand unutterable pleasures in tiring of certain works, and in finding their affection re-kindled for others.   They look back with a kind of tenderness to the time when they surfeited them-selves with Chopin through exclusive devotion to the *Nocturnes* and *Polonaises,* and remember how the *Preludes* and *Études* gradually restored them to an unclouded affection.   Their choice is slow among those they love, and they sometimes see predilec-tions, that had seemed indispensable to them, fade away suddenly.   For life, too, presses upon them. Their soul is subject to change, also their heart, and esteem is an insufficient protection against being forsaken.

They have their days, for nothing is fixed, and they have to reaccustom themselves.   They even have days when all music is intolerable to them, except that which is said to be bad.

They are not ashamed to confess it and readily agree that sometimes this *valse lente,* or that worth-less tune, is not unbearable to them.   More than that, they will admit that it gives them a certain pleasure, if the surroundings are favourable to it, or if their own state of mind desires it.   They obstinately believe that a good *czardas* is worth more than a bad quartet.

In France we are passing through a period that is incomparable for music.   We rave about it, we discuss it, we compose it, certainly in too great profusion, but the elect will recognise their own. There is no need to be anxious about it. Let us on the contrary admire how, among so many musical works, those which possess merit have quickly reached the little group of amateurs which, from the very first, decides what is to endure of a period.

There is as much to discover in the past as in the future. Let us look to the right or the left, before us or behind, as fancy dictates. The important thing is to discover, to start on excursions with eyes that are free from fatigue, and to find in the most familiar subjects a little of ourselves in a new colour.

The chief aim is to pursue thus our journey with love, and to arrive at music, not as the fulfilment of an ungrateful and uninspired task, but, according to the moment, with tender feeling, with firm confidence, or with eager desire.

There is a time for confidences and a time for prayer. There is a time for conversation and for charming and frivolous discourse. Music has all these moments. The essential is to learn to yield to the forms that it is pleased to assume, and not to flatter ourselves that we may subject it to our own caprice.

A WORD ON MASSENET

IT seems to be very difficult to come to an understanding on this subject. Can we not, however, attempt to agree once and for all, now that a thousand matters of debate are disposed of which incited envy or contempt during his lifetime ?

There was a time when, in our concern for pure music and for less facile developments, we rose against Massenet, and especially against the æsthetics for which he stood in the eyes of his uncompromising admirers.   There is no occasion to-day to retract our former opinion in full, but we need to understand one another.   The strength of the opposition to be offered to certain works must be measured by the extent of their influence.   The death of Massenet and the evolution of music in France render superfluous the energetic manifestations of which our youth was not the sole cause.

Formerly Auber, who knew what he was talking about, said that nothing fades so quickly as music. He intended to refer to that of the theatre, since that was almost the only music that met with appreciation in his day.   It is true that nothing loses its colour so much as the charm of the lyric drama, even when it is of excellent quality.   To be sincere, we cannot deny that we experience a certain feeling of tedium even in listening to *Dardanus* or *Alceste*.   The charm of the *Barber of Seville*, however attractive it still may be, has lost some of its colour. There is in reality only Mozart who survives the passing centuries.   He had the genius of youth, and so big a heart that we have not exhausted it.

Besides points of issue which are dimmed by the passage of time, there are the passions which a work may have let loose, for reasons, strictly speaking, connected with æsthetics.

Thus the same minds which, twenty years ago, were passionately Wagnerian, found themselves compelled to modify their ardour ten years later, and even to develop a new resistance, the reason being that the young French school had no further need to seek guidance in Wagnerism, having exhausted those of its elements which lent themselves to assimilation and was ripe, in its turn, to lead its own life. A continued affection, nourished on such fare, would have incurred a very real danger of developing into servility.

The movement of which Massenet is the leader is equally capable of explanation, although it cannot be compared to that to which Wagner gave rise. The antipathy aroused ten years ago by the rabid and wide-spread cult of an insipid melodic style must give way to-day to a moderate degree of sympathy, qualified with reservations here and there yet sincere and devoid of unnecessary indulgence.

There is really no need to make use of a man or a work as a weapon against innovators, and there is something rather humorous in seeing ignorant fanatics attack the composer of *Pelléas et Mélisande* in the name of the composer of *Werther*, when Claude Debussy himself, unlike the Debussyists, has never feared to bear witness that he retained much more than an idle esteem for Massenet's music.

We are certainly not going to agree with those for whom Massenet represents the summit of lyrical sincerity and musical intelligence. But why should the warm affection and deep admiration we feel for Debussy and Dukas, for *Pelléas* and *Ariane*

et Barbe Bleue, deprive us of the right to continue
to take pleasure in *Werther* and *Esclarmonde,* or
in certain passages of *Grisélidis,* and to consider
Le Jongleur de Notre-Dame as one of the master-
pieces of *opéra-comique* of the last century in France?

When it is desired to extol to us the sincerity of
Thaïs, or the atmospheric truth of *Hérodiade,* we
really can no longer follow, for the absence of all
fundamental truth, the unbridled desire to please,
the languorous insipidity of a conventional emotion
are to be felt in every part of such works. Massenet
had the theatrical sense developed to a degree the
more rare, insomuch as he makes no use of the more
blatant means. He is always able to retain a degree
of distinction that is indisputable even when it is
only relative. He has yielded no more to noisy
realism than he has attempted to attain to lofty
grandeur. He was aware of what must be termed
his own mediocrity. None knew its limitations
better than he. He has rarely attempted to trans-
cend his own powers except in *Ariane* and in *Bacchus,*
and again in *Roma,* but that was when age had
already affected him, though he did not visibly
show it. When he concerned himself with the Faith
he selected *Marie-Madeleine.* His conception has,
however, little that is religious, and suggests the
courtesan of modern Paris rather than of the historic Gospels. To realise his dream of Mary Mag-
dalen he went to the *quartier de l'Europe* and left
to others the little shops of Saint-Sulpice.

The tedium of certain bombastic works that some
are seeking to set up in opposition to these has

caused a less restive sympathy to revive in us. Our affection is relative, as was our antipathy.

It is easy to foresee a near future in which his works will have little more interest than those of Meyerbeer to-day ; but they will not have less, and they will possess in addition a certain charm, and a really musical feeling that was always lacking in the composer of *Les Huguenots*.

Their merits differ, but, for reasons equally governed by the stage, they will meet with the same fate.

When one remarks that in the French provinces, out of twenty performances in an operatic season, no less than ten are devoted exclusively to Massenet's operas, one is entitled to conclude that it is really going too far. But when it is desired to slaughter us with dramas that are gloomy, languid, and musically tedious, and when a writer is only admitted to the lyric drama on condition that he dons the shoes of Wagner, or even only his slippers, then we say with emphasis: " We prefer Massenet."

When it is attempted to reduce him to the level of a Leoncavallo, or a Puccini, we must rebel at all cost. We do not demand for him the throne of the true Immortals, but a stool is too little.

His works can no longer exercise a disastrous influence on the new generation. Those who wish to imitate him achieve only insipidity where he infused charm, and they outdo unbearable defects. Massenet produced some Massenet that was too bad for us to need more of it. As for good Massenet, he alone knew how to write it. To others belong the exquisite, the rare, and the powerful, but he had a delectable supineness.

To sum up, even if we have lost the desire to hear them again, let us admit that some of his works are excellent of their kind.

GABRIEL FAURÉ

NONE stands nearer to the masters by whom we are most deeply stirred : Chopin, Schumann, or Schubert ; yet none is more French.   His emotional quality retains a sense of proportion that always reveals his ability to discriminate.   That is not to say that it contracts.   On the contrary, it is the highest quality of this inspiration that it always gives an impression of freedom and yet never transgresses the limits set by the most exacting taste.

At a time when the majority of musicians have given their attention for preference to orchestral innovations, to discovering new resources of sound, or to resuscitating in more vivid form the French inclination towards the picturesque in music, Gabriel Fauré has remained chiefly attached to the riches of the piano or of song, and to the inexhaustible inflections of the melodic line.   To the latter he has given a shape that bears his obvious stamp, however varied its sensitive traceries.

Fauré's melody is always safeguarded from banality no less than from oddity.   It breathes irresistible freshness and youth.   Others there may be of greater suavity, suggesting an angelic approach, but among us there is none who makes us feel so well the charm of earth and of life.

The strong fragrance of the mornings, the languor and sweet serenity of the evenings nourish his emotional confidences. He has furnished more than a hundred poems, selected from the best of our time, with irreproachably appropriate commentary. He is able to penetrate to the heart of the poet himself and transmute his most secret intentions for the purposes of music.

The songs of Gabriel Fauré are caskets which are devoid of glitter, but retain within them the perfume of the most fastidiously refined soul, inspired with frank emotions and with discreet melancholy. Open them a little and we are penetrated with their charm. Reopen them often and we can realise how inexhaustible is that charm.

This quality of charm, the highest because it is truly the most complete in our nation ; this quality, of which some have believed that Massenet alone had the secret, so far as music is concerned, we well know Fauré to possess to a degree to which none since Couperin or Dandrieu has been able to attain in France. In Massenet the charm had too much languor, too many affectations, and it often skirted doubtful contacts. He was always too well aware of what he was coming to. In his coquetry the paint was often visible, and, as compared with a few enduring accents, how much has he become aged already by this desire to please that obsessed him beyond all measure !

The charm of Fauré is that he does not trouble so much about winning our approval as about satisfying his own heart and his own mind, which is unconcerned with what is popular. He has no disdain for others, nothing that is scornful or strained, but he is always able, with intention, to disclose or withhold himself.

The delight of this charm consists precisely in the absence of all feeling of constraint, and he makes no greater effort to beguile us at all cost than he does to evade the wishes of the vulgar. No touch could be more sure, nor could one impart the feeling of a more unconfined, voluptuous pleasure.

There are impulses, revulsions, affections and avowals, insinuations and troubled sighs, as of a conscience unburdening itself, youthful joys and radiant awakenings. Which of us can hear, without being overwhelmed with youthful feeling, the opening of the sonata, or the last song of *La Bonne Chanson*, and who can listen to *Le Don Silencieux* without being gently touched to the quick in the innermost of his dearest memories?

Had he no other merit, would it not be a considerable one to have endowed French music with an accurate and profound conception of the true song? If we possess to-day a marvellous flower-garden wherein music and poetry mingle their imperishable perfumes for our delectation, let us not forget that it was Gabriel Fauré who opened the gate and disclosed to our wonder-stricken gaze the fragrant beauty of this French garden. Each of these songs is perfectly constructed, but, even more than in their design and in their colour, does their value consist in the subtlety of their atmosphere, varied according to the subject treated. *Clair de Lune, Les Roses d'Ispahan, Présents, Automne, Soir,* create, without the paltry study of local colour, the desired frame for our emotions. It is from the sentiment itself that the appropriate atmosphere radiates and suavely envelops the subject, thanks to an exhaustible wealth of harmony.

Even when cast in the utmost simplicity, the fulness of these musical poems is ever present. The picture is never dwarfed by the frame. Their shape and their dimensions are so accurate that at first they pass unnoticed. Fauré's art proceeds by infinitesimal nuances. The most minute inflection suffices with him to give a varied impression of himself. Most of all do his conclusions beguile us. They are seldom categorical. The manner in which they are reached is sometimes the last we should have expected, but this is contrived, not for the pleasure of taking us by surprise, but rather in order to leave us regretting the end, and for the secret joy of a precarious conclusion. There is no musician who knows so well how to close without concluding, and yet not leave the mind irritated, but, on the contrary, offer it the enjoyment of agreeable sounds gently lapsing into silence.

It is an art imbued with unfailing elegance of the kind that is born not merely of fashion, but of an intimate distinction, and which makes no parade of its novel refinements but wears them as a habit made of niceties, discretion, and charm.

F

Some there were who doubted whether such art was capable of attaining to greatness. They had failed to grasp that true elegance needs little more than this to display itself in the form of the truest nobility, of which *Pénélope* furnishes the proof.

By means as simple as those of Racine himself, and therefore by paths other than those by which power is sought, he unfolded before us a drama of unique quality, which is without any of the coldness of those who tax their ingenuity to make tracings of Homer or Euripides without regard for the vitality that is the first essential. There was an austere splendour in this evocation, whose greatness came from a mind that borrows no powers save from the emotion that radiates from within towards all things suited to it.

The sure touch of Gabriel Fauré moves us because it has never the pretension to provoke our wonder It never adopts with us the accents of peremptory assurance. With how much greater ardour do we, feeling ourselves free, follow such music than that of the imperious kind, of which there is so much.

This music leads us towards unforeseen revolutions, but with such ease that it gives us only enjoyment, and never lets us feel the insidious tone of a sarcasm, or of a perverse satisfaction in leading us where we did not expect. We follow it without fear as without fluster.

There is no music that is more French. It fuses delightfully the elements of a skilful spontaneity. It is animated with smiles and perfumed with tender

tears. It is modelled on the heart which directs
and controls it. It never shouts, and we hear it all
the better ; and sometimes it has much humour,
of the purest kind.

One need only hear the sonata to be convinced
of it. There is no sonata that is less dogmatic.
From this point of view it can be compared only
to those of Grieg, but Fauré's is French and does us
much belated honour. There is no sonata that is
less a sonata in the sense insisted upon by the gentlemen of the gauge and the ruler. One might take
it for a *divertissement*, a phantasy. It has not the
pretension, like some others, of containing a treatise
of metaphysics, or the solution of the social problem.
It is simply music. That is a miracle which is far
from happening to all sonatas.

Already thirty-five years have passed over the
Quartet in C minor without lessening its charm or
dissipating its fragrance. By this work chamber-
music in France won, at the time of its first efforts,
its right to endure. It still appears to us to-day
decked in exquisite youth and in the bloom of its
first novelty. Of such works are also the other
Quartet, the *Quintet*, and the *Ballade*.

In each of these works, all holds together with a
mysterious cohesion. The reason is that nothing
in them is done to seize our attention. Everything
fulfils its form. There are no excrescences to aston-
ish or stupefy. I doubt if even Rameau's great
principle of concealing art by means of art itself
has ever been more thoroughly applied. No further
example is required than the touching *Requiem*.

But there is in the works of Gabriel Fauré an entire section that is less familiar, and yet fully impregnated with his highest qualities. It is that of his compositions for the piano. Their difficulty may have curbed unskilled ardour. Yet our day is one in which difficulties are made light of, and even abused. The true reason of the lack of appreciation they have met with is that they have not the picturesque allurement of so many happy examples of modern French music in which the piano serves as a favourable stage for evocations, for fairy-like scenes, for enchanted sights. Gabriel Fauré has written only *Preludes, Nocturnes, Impromptus, Barcarolles,* according to the custom consecrated by the genius of the masters of the piano. But he has succeeded in enclosing in them a feeling of the present. That is not so well known as it ought to be. Who in France really suspects that, for example, the sixth and seventh *Nocturnes* are masterpieces worthy to rank with the most beautiful movements in music ? None others can surpass them in skill. All in them is achieved with adroit sureness, and all unfailingly serves to express powerfully, or delicately, the richest emotions.

Though at the head of our national Conservatoire, Gabriel Fauré has not been given the prominence which is his due. The wide extent of his work has not yet been appreciated. Because he has devoted himself to the composition of chamber music at a time when above all the orchestra incites endeavours and successes, there has been a temptation to see in him a composer of less importance. Yet in the sight of immortality in music, Chopin is the equal of Liszt.

He has not known the triumphs that theatrical conquests award to some, and the indisputable success of *Pénélope* has happily kept within the precise limits that were appropriate to the composer's record and to our grateful joy, but he is the real master of the day. M. Saint-Saëns, who was Fauré's teacher, might have become that, but he has too often proved how little appreciation he has for French music apart from himself. It has pleased him to take up a scowling or aggressive attitude towards young musicians. He had the right to adopt it. We have the right to take no notice of it, and to find further pleasure in the knowledge that Gabriel Fauré's pupils include Florent Schmitt, Maurice Ravel, Roger-Ducasse, and that their affectionate friendship for such a master agrees with their varied temperaments, directed into different channels.

Enamoured of youth and of life, he has seen youth and life render him a homage which will be found to increase as the years pass by.

His works are one of the clearest and most precious of the mirrors in which may be seen reflected the varied and touching features of French music.

CLAUDE DEBUSSY

THERE is, in French contemporary art, scarcely an intellect in which are more clearly gathered together, or graven in deeper relief, the qualities

and characteristics most appropriate to our race.
Works more strongly stamped with the impression
of a French form of excellence do not exist in literature, or in painting ; and music, though revealing
more than one valid effort to give free expression
to our national spirit, could not put forth the manifestations of our essential qualities with greater
clearness.

When they are mental qualities they are not
always visible to everybody, and there are unfortunately more to be met with who mislead than who
enlighten us concerning our true characteristics.
That is how French criticism for a considerable
period, which has not yet come to an end, was
occupied in showing that it did not in the least
grasp the traditional aspect of Debussy's music.

Truth to tell, never since Rameau has a French
work aroused so much passion as was displayed by
the French public in attacking or defending Debussy
during the last ten years. Ordinarily such ex-
plosions were reserved for foreign works, and many
blazed up on behalf of Rossini or Wagner who would
not have dreamed of becoming so busily active
concerning Chabrier or Lalo.

The obstinacy of Debussy's adversaries, no less
than the tenacity of his partisans, proves to the
least informed mind from the outset that we are
not in the presence of a simple construction of fashion,
and that contemporary snobbism is not responsible
for such enthusiasm, as was very stupidly main-
tained by a certain " thinker."

Let us at once take into consideration that

Debussy was of all people the least in a position to lend his own support to the agitations that gathered round his works and his theories. At a time when friendships and social obligations appear to be the factors not only of success but even of artistic activities, there are few who have succeeded so well in retaining their addiction to solitude, or who have held so constantly aloof from all polemics, from all discussion of the ideas of the present day or those of to-morrow. The interested, sly, and at the same time indifferent, relations which constitute ordinary Parisian friendships are nothing to him. Even in musical circles there are many who are unfamiliar with his personal appearance and acquainted only with the inaccurate representation of it given by Jacques Blanche's portrait.

One could only be astonished at finding that his habitual solitude had not given rise to more legends and errors concerning him, as it has done for so many others. But the quality of his music has diverted from his person the untimely curiosity of the Press, and Claude Debussy knows, from a brief passage through journalism, that it is advisable to put some distance between himself and the chatter of reporters.

In reality, no wit is more attractive than his, for those who are not only interested in serious matters, but who appreciate with enjoyment the play of paradox. The articles which Claude Debussy wrote formerly on music in the *Revue Blanche* [1]

---

[1] A portion of these articles, slightly revised, forms the contents of a little volume published by M. Dorbon, *aîné*, under the title, *Entretiens avec M. Croche*.

are an interesting record of the paradoxical irony of his thought. But if they are examined more closely one cannot fail to discern in them the clearness of his vision, the subtlety of his feeling, and, behind flashes of irony, the warmth of enthusiasms that remain hidden through a distaste for self-assertion, and for words which use has rendered commonplace.

These traits are none other than those which set a deep mark upon the least of his musical expressions, and, having been some time in contact with him, one cannot fail to appreciate the fine co-ordination of his work with his mind.

It is true that some have found pleasure in reproaching this music with morbidness and neurasthenia. The neurasthenia of Debussy is another suggestion as ridiculously stupid as the allegations of decadence made against Henri de Régnier or Francis Jammes. This is not the place to quote once again the classic preface written by Gautier for the *Fleurs du Mal*, but one would seek in vain in this subtle, delicate, sensuous, strong and impassioned music for a trace of morbidness or suspicious lassitude. Certainly Claude Debussy has not escaped the spirit of the times, or even certain fashions, obsolete to-day, which constituted symbolism, but these fashions themselves affect no more than the surface of his earliest works, and the charm which one can still enjoy in them to-day bears excellent witness that they are unconcerned with an ephemeral fashion.

Claude Debussy was musically educated in the

precepts of the national Conservatoire.   He achieved
distinction there in some of the tasks which fill the
modest " work-basket " of aspirants for the *Prix
de Rome*.   He gained this prize in 1884, having been
prepared for it by the skilful and sceptical teaching
of Guiraud.   It appears that he brought back from
Rome only a more lively disdain for academic
favours, for the spirit of established institutions,
and for the recipes according to which musical
pastry is manufactured to gratify the palate of
crowds.

The clearly defined personality which asserted
itself in Claude Debussy before his twentieth year,
and which acquired a sharper outline as time went
on, caused him to be considered, by most of those
who had wind of his earliest writings, an artist of
isolated type; but the taste for mediocrity, which
is customary in the public, causes every strong and
individual artist to appear isolated until, with the
aid of years, it is discovered that by none was the
tradition better represented.

The same happens with tradition, as with certain
rivers whose course is lost for a time in some cleft
only to reappear unexpectedly further on. Sometimes its new direction seems to give ground for
denial that it is the same stream.

The French musical tradition is, in the history
of art, one of the most vivid examples of developments which circumstances combined to obstruct.
Ignorance of our past made the way easy for foreign
influences, alternately Italian and German.   The
works of Gluck, Rossini, Meyerbeer, and Wagner

in turn imposed inflections upon our music which were not indigenous to it, and could only adapt themselves to our musical thought by weakening its character. For those who will come later to study the movement of musical thought, the coalition of efforts directed, towards 1875, to the rejuvenation of French musical expression, or rather the liberation of a truly French form of music from the midst of foreign importations which submerged it, will be one of the most singular and engrossing spectacles.

We were reminded once that at the opening of the performances, directed by Charles Bordes, at which the singers of Saint-Gervais revived the wonderful treasure of the French composers of the fifteenth and sixteenth centuries, one of the most constant and most interested listeners was precisely Claude Debussy. Since then we have seen in his works, by the *Chansons de France* for four voices ; by the *Hommage à Rameau* ; by the employment of the modes of the Gregorian chant in *Pelléas* ; by the articles in the *Revue Blanche*, that Debussy held our old French masters to be much more his predecessors than, for example, Schumann or Wagner.

This was no mere archaistic taste or imitative instinct. Among French composers of to-day he is really one of those who take the least interest in the historical study of music. His musical learning and his curious studies were guided much more by the demands of his feelings than by musicographical prescription.

But, like these charming old masters, he has a soul sensitive to the minutest harmonic vibrations. Like them he has the sense of the picturesque, the love of delicate polyphony, and a mode of expression varied in accordance with the inner direction of his feelings and not with the strict precepts of " development."

Having raised the cry of anarchy in presence of the works of Claude Debussy, envy now exhausts itself in denying him a great part of his originality, and transferring the credit for it back to diverse sources, particularly to the Russian composers. The performances of *Boris Godunoff* gave rise to suggestions of this kind, and, if it is permitted to recall a personal anecdote, I shall relate how, one evening when I was leaving Claude Debussy's house in a hurry, on purpose to go and hear *Boris*, the composer said to me with an expression of ironic pleasantry: " You are going to hear *Boris*. Ah! you will see. There is the whole of *Pelléas* in it."

He said that to me with a serious air; and the habitual irony of his glance, further enhanced at the moment, showed that he had full knowledge of the jealousies which surrounded him.

One ought, however, to have remembered that Claude Debussy had been one of the first in France to praise the masterpieces of the Russian School. One evening he even appeared on their behalf as pianist at a concert of the *Société Nationale*.

When he was still young, circumstances caused him to spend some time in Russia. Already fascinated by sonorities, his soul was attracted and

charmed by the curious modulations of the popular
themes from which all the beauty of that which
we call to-day the Russian School drew its nourish-
ment. The colour-impressionism of these themes
was fated to captivate him. The mode of vocal
expression adopted by the popular singers attracted
him.

It was impossible that the novelty of all this
should fail to make a considerable impression upon
this young brain. But it was all fused in the
natural expression of his genius, and, sifted through
a truly French intellect, acquired a new quality.

It would be as absurd to deny the Russian
influence in the foundation of the Debussyist mode
of expression as it is to say, as some do, that all
Debussy is in Musorgsky.

Before even going to Russia, Debussy had composed works which gave proof of an original mind
and a truly personal style, among others, *The
Blessed Damozel*, and some songs. Let us merely
recall that the Institut rebelled against the harmonic
innovations of the young " prix de Rome " as far
back as *Le Printemps*, the symphonic poem which
he sent from Rome in 1887, and which was refused
a hearing by the academicians then deputed to
preside over the evolution of art in France.

It would be interesting to be enabled to know
certain unpublished works, such as *Almanzor*, the
first work sent from Rome in 1889 immediately after
The Blessed Damozel. But there are songs, like
L'Ombre des arbres dans la rivière (in the *Ariettes
oubliées*), composed long before it was published,

which prove that Claude Debussy's originality stood in no need of foreign aid for its distinctive development.

From that day to the time of writing this chapter, the composer has merely given definite shape, little by little, to qualities that were revealed in his earliest pages. Are not the delicacy, the discretion, the colour, and the feeling that are displayed in *The Blessed Damozel*, the same features that we shall find reaffirmed and developed in *Pelléas et Mélisande*, in the *Nocturnes*, in *La Mer*, as well as in the *Prélude à l'après-midi d'un Faune*, or in the songs ?

If *Pelléas et Mélisande* has contributed the most to the fame of Claude Debussy, and if in truth that lyric drama is one of the composer's most lasting works, it is especially by his chamber music that the Debussyist enthusiasm was nourished and established at the very beginning.

Long before the appearance of *Pelléas* (1902) certain restricted groups of new music-lovers were studying the *Cinq Poèmes de Baudelaire*, the *Fêtes Galantes*, the *Chansons de Bilitis*, and the *Proses Lyriques*, which already represented nearly the whole output of the composer in song-form. The *Ariettes oubliées* and the second book of the *Fêtes Galantes* remained to be published soon after *Pelléas*.

Even to-day, when Claude Debussy has emerged as one of the foremost, and certainly one of the most alluring, symphonists in Europe, there are some who find joy in seeing him continue writing in the song form in which there are pages, old or recent, which count among the finest blossoms of a period rich above all others.

For thirty years we have assisted, in France, at a most marvellous efflorescence of songs. Art such as that of Gabriel Fauré, Castillon, Chausson, Henri Duparc, Pierre de Bréville, Charles Bordes, and, later on, Maurice Ravel, Déodat de Sévérac, Albert Roussel, Florent Schmitt, and Gabriel Grovlez, has endowed France with an aggregate of songs revealing the best aspects of French feeling, and permitting a delectable and charming union of poetry with music.

The thirty odd songs which constitute Debussy's output in this form remain among the finest, most subtle, and most varied productions of this period.

First of all, the simple consideration of the poems to which they were written reveals in the musician a well-informed literary sense, and an artistic taste more certain than had long governed composers in their choice of poems to set to music. But Debussy does not belong solely to the musical movement of his day. At the time of his first efforts, he moved in the circles in which was formed the literary æsthetic that vouchsafed us the most beautiful works of the close of the nineteenth century. He lived among young authors whose masters were Verlaine, and Mallarmé, whose gods were Baudelaire, and Villiers de l'Isle-Adam. His first compositions were issued by a literary publisher, at the *Librairie de l'Art Indépendent*, where Henri de Régnier, Pierre Louys, André Gide, and others met. The delicate mind of the composer, and his sensitive

and refined nature, could not fail to feel itself
attracted by the artistic aristocratism of the
intellectual disciples of Mallarmé. Thus he came
to apply himself to interpret in music the literary
thoughts of only the best authors. These were
Verlaine in the *Fêtes Galantes* and the *Ariettes
oubliées*; Rossetti in *The Blessed Damozel*; Mallarmé in the *Prélude à l'après-midi d'un Faune*;
and, finally, Maeterlinck in *Pelléas et Mélisande*.

Moreover, none was better qualified than Claude
Debussy to interpret the thoughts of these writers,
which were often elusive and mysterious, musical
and suggestive. The proofs he has given us of his
comprehension are really astonishing. When one
examines the musical interpretations of the *Cinq
Poèmes* or the *Fêtes Galantes*, one immediately
realises the care with which the composer has
endeavoured to transform the quality and the
substance of his music in accordance with the mind
of the poet. It is a wide distance from the gravity,
the strong and rich musical substance of *Recueillement*, or of *La Mort des Amants*, to the tender or
witty delicacies of the *Faune*, or *Fantoches*.

Some superficially minded people are inclined to
say, almost without having heard it, that Debussy's
music always resembles itself. To begin with, one
might retort that it thus retains the merit of not
resembling any other. But there is no reproach
less merited to be made against it than the charge of
monotony. One might as well accuse Baudelaire,
Verlaine, or Mallarmé. In reality, even taking into
consideration the great beauty of the songs of

composers like Chausson, Duparc, or Fauré, one may assert that none has surpassed Debussy in the intelligence of the musical commentary to a poem. No page of Baudelaire has been more subtly evoked than *Recueillement* or *Le Jet d'Eau*, and if one listens to the ten or so poems of Verlaine which the composer has illustrated, one cannot fail to realise how the tender, languorous phrasing of *C'est l'extase*, the rumbling and deep rhythm of *Le Faune*, the impish spirit of the *Fantoches*, the melancholy of the delightful theme in *Spleen*, the rhythmic suppleness of *Chevaux de Bois*, all these diverse themes and diverse atmospheres, created by harmonic underlays—how they all prove not only the subtle intelligence of the composer, but the musical resourcefulness of the personality that is, perhaps, the most responsive that has ever been met with since the origins of music, and susceptible to the least modulations of the universe.

All the sense of the play of atmospheric colour, the feeling of the mysterious, the desire to suggest rather than describe, the obsession with the infinite mobility of light, that are covered by the word " impressionism," are characteristic of his works, or at least of the earliest of them.

It is thus not by mere technical gifts, by mere harmonic innovations, that Claude Debussy has justly deserved to be regarded as one of the greatest musicians of France, and the most alluring musical genius of contemporary Europe. It is by qualities of feeling, by the marvellous harmony between his musical style and the goal to which he aspires, by the most secure adaptation of his musical language to the emotions it is intended to excite. No musician has penetrated further on the path towards the suggestion of the mysterious and the intangible. His gentle, delicate, and often strange, harmonies release within us a thousand secret springs that no other music could reach. In proof of this we need only cite the emotion of all who have heard *Pelléas et Mélisande*, and felt the irresistible and ever singular charm of several scenes, particularly that in the castle vaults ; that of the tower where Mélisande smooths her hair at the window ; and that poignant scene of the death of Pelléas, in which there is no noisy shock to the ear, and whose strength proceeds not from the volume of the orchestra, but from the great accumulation of emotion contained within that anguished atmosphere of anxious passion, and of hatred whose conflict finds its end in death.

As opposed to other musicians of our day, for example, Richard Strauss or Gustav Mahler, Claude Debussy does not overload his orchestra. He obeys the French law of style which demands the maximum of expressiveness with the minimum of means. We have suffered the Wagnerian influence and the abuse of its expressive violence so long in France, that we can hardly disentangle the idea of power from the notion of orchestral volume. The character of Debussy's work lies in the quality of the tone-colours, in the infinite variety and extreme subtlety of tonality, but also in its profoundly human accents. For that even the orchestra is not

G

necessary. A few instruments suffice Debussy for the adequate expression of his harmonic subtlety.   He does not need more than a single instrument to prove his marvellous symphonic gift, and his piano-writing reveals a colourist who, continuing the French tradition of picturesque music, has given to it a brilliance and a quality that surpass even the delightful works of composers like Couperin or Rameau.

It is especially in his three last sets of pieces [1] that Debussy's piano-writing shows itself original, strong, and moving. The titles alone suffice to indicate their descriptive and suggestive intentions : *Pagodes*, *Soirée dans Grenade*, *Jardins sous la pluie*, *Reflets dans l'eau*, *Cloches à travers les feuilles*, *Poissons d'or*, and so on. But only a frequent and attentive hearing can reveal their full emotional power.

Its fluidity is the cause that his music lends itself better than any other to the suggestion of water. It is a theme which Claude Debussy holds in affection and to which he owes some of his finest pages, such as *Jardins sous la Pluie*, the symphonic sketches *La Mer*, or the adorable scene at the spring in *Pelléas*.

It is impossible for minds, or even for feelings, that are not enthralled by a narrow religion of the past, to avoid yielding to all the charm, the suggestive truth, and the intellectual sensuousness that is

[1] The two books of " Preludes," which comprise some of the composer's finest pages, were published more recently than the date of this article.

contained in pieces like *La Soirée dans Grenade* or that short but strangely impressive page that is entitled *Et la lune descend sur le temple qui fut.*

Claude Debussy's music will ever be opposed by those who demand at all cost that a musical work shall prove something, as if a work of art served some end other than beauty for its own sake. Claude Debussy has had the good fortune to free French music once more from all these philosophical, metaphysical, or moral pretensions upon which German music is too often nourished. That such aims conform to Teutonic genius is undeniable, but they are as remote as possible from French genius.

French music has had no national character, or nearly none, for a century. The nationalisation of music in France is not the work of Debussy alone ; it is a movement of ideas that has been taking place for thirty years or more, and to which the best musical intellects have contributed, but none has approached the thesis of a truly French musical spirit with more striking proofs and a more clear-seeing conscience than Claude Debussy.

Through him there has been a return of clear, delicate, expressive, and emotional feeling, of the intellectual quality and supple spirit that is as appropriate to tenderness as to a smile : in short, all that is characteristic of the true precursors of present-day music, the old minstrels equally with our masters of the Renaissance, our clavecinists from Chambonnières to Dandrieu, and also Jean-

Philippe Rameau. There is between them and Claude Debussy the difference that is inherent to the evolution of centuries, but one and all give, as do our works of literary and plastic art, the standard of that which is commonly termed the French genius.

This art is not lowered by being claimed as French. Despite those who assert that music is a universal art, it is permissible to believe that perhaps none other has given better proof of race, and that does not by any means exclude the universal interest or affection that may accrue to it. In spite of all, Schumann and Wagner are German musicians. The soul of Norway vibrates in the music of Grieg, as does that of Hungary in the music of Liszt. Musorgsky asserts the Russian character as clearly as Haydn, Schubert, and Mahler the various aspects of the Viennese spirit, and we find in their presence varied and deep enjoyment.

The reception that Claude Debussy encountered out of France proves that this French spirit by its genius touches the essence of the modern soul. The success of *Pelléas et Mélisande* at Milan, New York, Brussels, Cologne, and the triumph that acclaimed it in London ; the discerning articles written on his music in England, Germany, Italy, and Spain ; the nearly always enthusiastic affection that it arouses in different places ; and even the adversaries this music has incited ; are they not so many unexceptionable admissions of its greatness and of its beauty ?

(1909)

CONCERNING A BOOK ON
CLAUDE DEBUSSY

WHILST articles, pamphlets, lectures, and books on the composer of *Pelléas et Mélisande* were multiplying abroad, particularly in England, no French volume had yet been devoted in its entirety to our compatriot. Yet the abundance and the quality of his works, the maturity and solidity of his best productions, had indicated for some time that it might be legitimate and profitable to speak of Debussy's music, not in the terms of final analysis, but with some certainty of his decisive directions.

Assuredly it is still too soon (and we cannot but rejoice in the fact) to aim at giving a definite picture of his work. Claude Debussy's maturity is certainly not yet in its decline. We still await *La Chute de la Maison Usher*, *Le Diable dans le Beffroi*, and the *Histoire de Tristan*, from which we hope, amid the regrets of disillusioned Wagnerians, to acquire new grounds for affectionate attachment to the genius of our race. In the absence of a more complete picture there was, however, need to dedicate to his fame more than the somewhat furtive homage of our review articles.

There is a charming moment in the fame of a great mind that disdains fame, when his accomplishment as yet includes among its admirers only fervent and considered enthusiasm. It is the moment when the solitude of almost unanimous failure to understand is coming to an end, and when the era of unreasoned and fashionable admiration is only dawning. The fame of Claude Debussy is commencing to traverse this phase of transition. This is the moment when Debussyists of the earliest days will feel some irritation at hearing all and sundry speak at random of a master who was long disparaged.

Already there are people of fashion who experience that it is no longer advisable to deride, and that it is seemly to add some sympathy for the composer of *Jardins sous la Pluie* to their admiration for Puccini, Massenet, or Rodolphe Berger.

Let us treat this kind of admiration with contempt. We know how much it is worth per yard. And let us rejoice once more that the voluntarily aloof personality of Debussy almost completely silences the newspaper instinct for gossip. Already, apart from certain circles where one truly lives on beauty and on artistic curiosity, it has become unbearable to speak of French music, because one so invariably knocks against disconcerting forms of eclecticism. Abroad, one may still find some pleasure in it. In the course of giving lectures in Switzerland, in Belgium, and especially in England, I have been able to verify the ardour and sincerity of foreign Debussyists. There are still others elsewhere. Barcelona has a number of them. Ildebrando Pizzetti voiced in Italy the opinions of some young men whom the æsthetics of M. Leoncavallo or of M. Mascagni failed to satisfy. If they are more rare in Germany, they are not less ardent, and I will wager that M. Louis Laloy's work on our composer will be welcomed with even greater benefit abroad than in France.

M. Laloy's personality justifies and gives authority to this book. It is already long since he repeatedly manifested his reasoned admiration for the composer of the *Estampes* in the *Mercure Musical*, and later in *S. I. M.* His articles, among others, on *La Mer*, and on the *New Manner of Claude Debussy*, remain among the best contributions to the Debussyist bibliography. His intimacy with the musician in no wise detracts from the value of a sagacious and sure criticism, and permits, on the contrary, a stricter survey of his work.

M. Laloy's book appeared in a collection destined not for professionals, but for cultivated and fastidious amateurs. One would therefore look through it in vain for any technical indication or formal analysis. He has wisely preferred to set himself to deduce the spirit that governs this alluring music, raises it above its own period, and ensures its survival. Besides, it would be an injustice were the works of Debussy allowed to become a subject exclusively for musicians. Most of these have been the last to understand the work of their colleague. I do not speak of the youngest, nearly all of whom maintain a lively and sincere admiration for this music. But, apart from Messager and Fauré on the one hand, and Vincent d'Indy on the other, most of the composers of the preceding generation have given this newcomer no more than a pitying smile. Some endeavour to-day, not always without clumsiness, to repair their former error—but who is deceived ?

The most sincere admirers of Claude Debussy

from his first appearance were writers and painters who were not shocked by the technical liberties contained in his works, but allowed themselves to be captivated by their delicate and powerful charm without carrying their analysis beyond the limits of their intimate feelings.

Those who may attempt to consider Debussy's music independently of the literary period in which it appeared will have only an incomplete and mistaken idea of the composer. This explains why his works still give much more general pleasure to art-lovers than to musicians reared upon classicism. The works of the German romantics, or those of Berlioz, were not steeped to this extent in the literary atmosphere of their day.

To-day, when the bonds of music and letters have not relaxed, but rather the reverse, there is no music that represents more fully an æsthetic period than did in their own day the group formed by such sets of song as *Fêtes Galantes* (first book), *Cinq Poèmes*, and such symphonic pieces as the *Prélude à l'après-midi d'un Faune*, or the *Nocturnes*.

The conversations held in Bailly's shop, at the *Librairie de l'Art Indépendent*, where met the most original spirits of the younger literature, did not fail to determine, or rather play their part in revealing, the æsthetic soon afterwards displayed in *Pelléas et Mélisande*. In this it is not so much a question of an influence of literature on the composer, as of an atmosphere which was, towards 1890, common to all minds possessing artistic curiosity. Claude Debussy's originality was born at the same time as that of these writers, it developed from the same causes, and its roots were deep and personal.

Many facts, moreover, prove the precocity with which it was formed. To tell the truth, it is not in the *prix de Rome* cantata, *L'Enfant Prodigue*, that one could discover the real Debussy. When one recalls the true spirit of the young composer at this date, one receives the impression of a clever hoax. There are in *L'Enfant Prodigue* only vague corners in which a personal spirit is shown. Most of it has a melodic facility that certainly sets one thinking more of Massenet than of *Pelléas et Mélisande*. The airs of Azraël and of Lia strike the insipid note of a commonplace musicality devoid of real emotion.

What causes one to think that this was only the voluntary exercise of a well-informed student who knew with what sauce one tickles the palate of certain gentlemen of the Institut, is a very curious song in the *Ariettes oubliées* : *L'ombre des arbres dans la rivière*. This song, which is already penetrated with the true Debussy spirit and has the musical outlines dear to its author, was written four years before the *prix de Rome*. Further proof is that two years after the *prix de Rome* he wrote the exquisite *Blessed Damozel* which, without being one of his important works, none the less remains one of the most characteristic.

Moreover, the second work that he sent home from Rome, the symphonic suite *Printemps* (1887), was considered by the Institut to be really insufficiently orthodox, and its performance was opposed, which led Debussy the following year to

refuse to allow a performance of *The Blessed Damozel*
unless *Printemps* were included in the programme.

M. Laloy gives another anecdote to confirm the
truth of this precocious formation. He informs us
that before the *prix de Rome* Claude Debussy, whilst
attending Guiraud's class at the Conservatoire,
brought to the latter a small score composed after
Banville's *Diane au Bois*. Guiraud said to him :
" Well, all that is very interesting, but you must
reserve it for later on, or you will never get the *prix
de Rome*." May Guiraud's name be rescued from
oblivion for that clear-seeing and sceptic remark !

No one will ever see this score of *Diane au Bois*.
It is to be regretted for the sake of the study of the
composer's intellectual development, and because
one may be assured that, from that moment, Claude
Debussy was already writing real Debussy music.

The character of his mind is so clearly impressed
that it could not fail to assert itself early, as the
independence of its intellectual attitude sheltered
him from taking counsel of the taste most in favour,
or making the slightest concession to it.

The mixture of assurance in the direction of his
work, and voluntary indolence in his opinions, is the
stamp of this uncommon figure. In him the most
sure and most refined sense of things is united to a
love of paradox. Through his personal qualities of
acute feeling and irony in discourse and in writing,
by his emotional delicacy and his strong clarity in
his works, Claude Debussy is at present one of the
minds most representative of our secret aspirations.

The ignorant antagonists of this music continue

obstinately to speak of the process, implying that
there is in this only a fashion that will pass away,
like American shoes or inordinately large feminine
hats. It is inevitable that technical questions must
be frequently discussed in days of artistic revolutions, but, unfortunately, the majority consider the
process as the essential and thus belittle the entire
work. For some time the same thing happened in
pictorial impressionism, and some are still met with
who think that the interest in the pictures of Monet
or Renoir consists chiefly in questions of pure tone
and the balance of complementaries, and who
similarly think that the interest in the coming of
Debussy arises from sequences of fifths or of ninths.
Apart from the fact that no process can claim to be
new, the " human " question is too often lost sight
of. Works of art do not exist solely for the use of
the mandarins, even if it is true that they are not
made for the crowd. Whether the latter be, from
the art standpoint, middle-class or popular, matters
little. But there are minds unequal to discuss
questions of technique and none the less sensitive to
the beauty of Elémir Bourges or André Gide ; of
Degas, Cézanne, or Marquet ; of Rodin or Aristide
Maillol ; of Dukas or Debussy.

Which of us has not felt, on hearing a work by
this composer, that the minds that were nearest to
its comprehension, and in any case most sensitive to
the emotion and the charm diffused by it, were not
always musicians, if by that we understand people
who have acquired more or less familiarity with the
solfeggio or the piano, perhaps even with harmony

and counterpoint, and are nourished on German
classics. It was these who, failing to find their sign-
posts in these works, taxed their ingenuity to pass
off Debussy's compositions as objects of curiosity,
lowering these sonorous constructions to the level
of mere *bric-à-brac*. Let us give credit to Louis
Laloy for having insisted with justice upon the
humanity of this music. Certainly Claude Debussy,
like his literary *confrères* in symbolism, may for a
time have inclined towards the somewhat exclusive
cult of the rare and the mysterious; but let us bear
in mind that the sense of musical dandyism never
came to weaken within him the quality of sincere,
communicative, and deep emotion. Let us recall
the opening and closing phrases of *Recueillement*, the
pure atmosphere of *The Blessed Damozel*, the singular
ardour of *La Chevelure*, and that is only to cite
works of remote date. Have we not repeatedly
experienced their penetrating and captivating charm,
devoid of bombast or of self-consciousness, or of
cosmetics ? If, now, this charm sometimes seems
to us a little thin, it is only because of the proximity
in our memories of more powerful and more moving
pages, such as the *Colloque Sentimental*, the dialogues
in *Pelléas et Mélisande*, or the delightful *Promenoir
des deux Amants*.

One can but agree without reservation with the
following utterance of Louis Laloy : " These works
were not only pages of beauty to be admired, but
they were friends always longed for, and endeared
to us by a secret melancholy. Born in deep solitude, they knew themselves to be offered up to the

impossible ; dedicated to absence ; and they expected no response to their tenderness. They were thoughtful virgins exiled on this earth. It was they who brought, and not to musicians alone, the message of a new alliance. There was in them a faith that exceeded the limits of a particular art, and there is a generation alive to-day in whom the *Nocturnes* and *Pelléas* have trained more than taste : the heart."

The great merit of Debussy is to have cherished grace, but not that form of it which was diffused in facile tunes by Massenet and the Italians, beloved of the crowd. It needed a sure taste, and more than the desire to please. But it was, in itself, a feat of daring, at a time of musical gravity that attained both to grandeur and to boredom, to think chiefly of pleasure ; and in doing so, to restore the link with the tradition of Couperin, Dandrieu, and Rameau, whose force consists of grace, whose evocations have not the pretension to do more than satisfy the taste of fastidious spirits, and prolong in our souls the simple and sincere emotion of their harmonious avowal.

Art is never so useless as when it sets out to be utilitarian and to serve another cause than that of freedom in life and that of beauty. Through having aimed at being social, metaphysical, or religious, with Wagner and César Franck, music was decking itself more and more in a depressing pedantry, reducing itself to the limits of a thesis, and to the narrowest processes of development. The art of pleasing cannot, however, be taught in twenty lessons. One cannot imagine without regret, or

without profound irritation, the music that Ernest
Chausson, for example, would have bequeathed us
had he been able to emancipate himself from the
scruples of the commandments which he imposed
upon himself during the whole of his life. He had
exquisite feeling, and was one of the first to understand in what degree literature and the graphic arts
could influence present-day music. None shows
more clearly than he the transition from Franckism
and Wagnerism to our present-day music. But he
lacked the courage to abandon himself to the
intellectual sensuousness he possessed within him,
and which preserved a strong and delicate beauty in
certain pages of his music.

An obsession of intellectual chastity, if one may
speak thus, weighed upon French music. Its
influence was doubly guilty, for music is the most
sensuous of the arts, and French music, moreover,
has never swerved from a sensuousness which may
perhaps constitute its weakness in the eyes of
German professors, but which, in our eyes, gives it
its grace, its truth, and its vitality, and preserves,
as fresh after two or three centuries as on the first
day, the pages of composers like Costeley, Couperin,
or Daquin.

There is not in the whole of music a more voluptuous mind than that of Claude Debussy. Always his
thought is bathed in the pleasures of sensation.
Sensitive to the least call of life, of nature, or of joy,
he skilfully prolongs within us the sometimes
melancholy sweetness of being conscious of our own
feelings, of our own life.

However, the element of strength has since then increased in his work with progressive sureness. Those who have followed the composer's development during the past ten years have rejoiced to see the traces of this melancholy, and all that it implied of a transitory nature, gradually diminish, and a real strength assert itself, which is always able to remain harmonious and true, and which constitutes the greatness of the last act of *Pelléas* as well as of the triptych *La Mer*.

Among French musicians there is none who has succeeded so well in balancing these two musical elements : charm and power—preserving the one from weakening into archness, and the other from lashing itself into violence. If it is true that one would seek in vain in his work for the will-power of *Salome* or the gripping force of *Boris Godunoff*, at least one feels in it nothing that is vulgar or insignificant. At least we feel within ourselves that this work comes from beyond the region of formulas and processes, however original these may be, and that it is born of the most perspicacious and refined sensibility, and, for us, the sensibility which corresponds the most to its object.

It is not easy to find, even among our authors, except perhaps in Henri de Régnier, a mind which reflects more accurately our race, or a more truly French figure. There is in it nothing that protrudes enormously ; all is delicately proportioned. It has unconstraint without vulgarity, emotion without grandiloquence. Let us not seek in this music for what can have no place in it by reason of its intentions, but, at this hour of revival in French music, is it truly possible to discover another mind capable of giving to our senses the measure of our qualities with greater charm or veracity?

And yet there is occasion to think that all aspects of his work have not yet been revealed. I am of those who are astonished at not yet finding more strongly accentuated in it the irony which is characteristic of him when expressing himself in literary form. The comic in music, musical irony, are modes of expression in which it seems to us that Claude Debussy should be equally capable of excelling, and forms of music which his qualities might with profit restore. Perhaps some day he will reward our expectation. Let us await *Le Diable dans le Beffroi*. Let us also await that *Histoire de Tristan* which, without diminishing the glory of Wagner's Teutonic *Tristan*, will restore to a French atmosphere, for our benefit, our beautiful and national legend, as was done in literature by Joseph Bédier.

We still have much to expect from a fertile and powerful mind which has already given us so much, and we must be grateful to those who, like Louis Laloy, by fixing for a moment our attention on this music, have given us sound reasons to cherish such hopes.

CONCERNING A MUSICAL COMEDY

MAURICE RAVEL'S *L'Heure Espagnole*

(*To Leon-Paul Fargue*)

WHATEVER may be the future of this charming and witty work, whatever fate will be meted out to it by a public that is perhaps too accustomed to gravity, and that has too often acquired the spirit of geometry at the expense of that of finesse, the performance of *L'Heure Espagnole*, which we had so long awaited and desired, will have stood for something more than a new opportunity of admiring one of the best musicians of to-day. It has furnished the occasion for considering the absorbing question of the comic spirit in music, absorbing, that is, at least for those whom the religion of seriousness at all costs has not deprived of some qualities that have at all times constituted the advantage and the charm of our race.

Long enough has a foreign sense of gravity influenced music in France. Nearly thirty years of effort are gradually liberating to-day our musical expression. The study of our true traditions haunts our writers on music, whilst the works of the finest intelligences in present-day music prove that its aims are justified.

Some years ago an enquiry on Wagner clearly revealed the spirit that governs music in France; and how right we are to rejoice to-day in a rivalry that endeavours to recreate a style of music appropriate to ourselves, such as we possessed in the

H

splendid time of the masters of the Renaissance, the delicate and sensitive period of our finest clavecinists.

It is not easy to disentangle oneself from foreign influences that have prevailed for more than a century. The tradition that had been broken by the Italianism of Rossini and the Germanism of Meyerbeer completed its submission to the genius of the great Germans. The romanticism of Schumann, rendered insipid by the excessive facility of Mendelssohn, aspired to represent French feeling and clearness. Liszt's sense of the picturesque, and the concentrated sensitiveness of Chopin, would surely have been better able to defend our essential qualities if these two masters had been better understood from the beginning.

A blow from the club of the Bayreuth Hercules imposed silence for a time on these legitimate claims. The spirit of the innovators could not disregard the merit of Wagner's works and the attractiveness of their æsthetic design. Gradually dramas like *Tristan* and *Parsifal* were discovered to have the quality inherent to masterpieces, but at the same time it was realised that the æsthetic revolution they were intended to assert was pure pretension.

The genius of César Franck, profoundly ingenuous, rallied round him an assemblage of young musicians, fascinated with abstract music and contemptuous of scenic conventions. But the Wagner-Franckist influence, in spite of being momentarily necessary, could not, without danger, continue to impose the weight of its metaphysics and of its instinctive religiousness. Debussyism, by its conscious spontaneity, its intellectual sensuousness, and the freshness of its impressions, naturally attracted those spirits that were anxious to hear music that would at least satisfy their desire to be charmed.

Too long had the taste for giving pleasure been despised and abandoned to facile manufacturers. We had turned aside from grace in the desire to be, above all, serious ; we seemed on the point of believing that, in music, the word " grace " should henceforth signify only a theological virtue.

The partisans of serious music, of theories, and of the " art of composing a sonata taught in twenty lessons," claimed that preciosity was the most terrible of all evils. In music the most terrible is boredom, and especially in France.

Unconcerned with these theorists, French feeling and the spirit and sense of the picturesque which govern its moods have created valid works which prove to the least prejudiced mind that the words " French music " are not vain, and that the qualities and defects of these musical works constitute perhaps the most national expression that the different arts can put forward at present in France.

The historian will assuredly have to rise above the petty quarrels, the rivalries, the rancours, or simply the temperamental divergences, which repeatedly rear themselves between the fanatics of the *Schola* and those who have discovered virtue in the

Conservatoire only after being formerly in contact with its narrow-mindedness.

In their essence, moreover, these divergences and conflicts only reveal a movement of ideas in search of more secure rules for its guidance.

It is undeniable, even for those who are the least informed on musical matters, that interest in music has never been so great in France as it is in our day, even if one recalls how great it was in the sixteenth century, or during the second half of the eighteenth.

On all sides we are assisting to-day at a reawakening of nationalities in music. To what cause are we to attribute it ? In the first place, perhaps, the organisation of musicographical research and the study of musical history may have led composers and audiences to a more adequate notion of our musical patrimony. Moreover, the spectacle of the national and popular character in Russian music may not have been without influence in inducing composers to consider the almost indefinite extent to which the personal quality in composition can derive sustenance from the songs of its native soil.

After Russia, England and Spain furnish us to-day with undeniable proofs of this reawakening of musical nationalities, of which there is already a suggestion also in Italy.

The sense of the picturesque, joined to the expression of a vivid and fastidious sensibility, and sometimes to evidences of a sense of humour, are the common measure of the works of Debussy, Ravel, Sévérac, Roussel, Schmitt, Roger-Ducasse, Grovlez, Caplet, Raoul Bardac, and others. At no other

time, perhaps, has France been so rich in disinterested effort and in ardent talent devoted to all
that has a relation to music. Some peevish minds,
after having denied all interest to the works of
Debussy, endeavour to represent the younger
French composers as so many emanations from the
master who composed *Pelléas*. Such tactics can
serve neither Debussy nor truth.

If Debussy's technical revolution could not fail to
impress its stamp upon our music of to-day, that
does not prevent individual feeling or intelligence
from expressing itself with originality.

It is true that one no longer feels between them
the existence of links such as those which for a time
created Wagnerism or Franckism. Are such links
really necessary ? In music, schools are of even less
utility than in the other arts.

Emanating more directly than any other art from
intimate feeling, music lends itself less readily to the
dogmatism of scholastic criticism. It reflects at
present, more fully even than literature or the
graphic arts, the individualism and the independence, or intellectual anarchy of our period, its
uncertainty, its anxiety, but also its vitality. For
that very reason it is the more difficult to determine,
as some would wish, whither tends our music.

During the whole of the time that the Wagnerian
influence lasted, we had the impression of knowing
whither we went, because the destiny and possibilities of music had been circumscribed by the
æsthetics of Bayreuth.

The personality of César Franck, in surrounding

itself with the best efforts of the younger composers about 1880-1890, had the appearance of containing the elements of a new æsthetic, whereas his teaching was, more accurately, limited to the noble example furnished by a fine artistic conscience. But could this religious genius, of such limited culture, aspire to direct for long the secret aspirations of a generation that was born in the full efflorescence of symbolism ?

Ernest Chausson seems to have been one of the first to have a presentiment of the extent to which the literature and painting of our period were about to penetrate musical expression, but the deplorable accident that cut short his life, in the fulness of its maturity, left us with this refined spirit represented only by works in which the feeling, which in him was original and subtle, was often thwarted by a certain dogmatism imposed upon it by exaggerated reverence. Since then musical works have shown a constant concern with literary or pictorial elements. This seems to conform closely to the genius of our race, since it is equally manifested in Goudimel or Jannequin, and in Couperin, Rameau, or Dandrieu. It is characteristic of nearly all the attractive works at whose unfolding we have assisted for more than ten years.

In default of knowing, as some demand, whither our music is progressing, we can at present enlighten ourselves more effectively concerning its true origins. One may have feared for a moment that the cult of the picturesque might dwindle into too exiguous curiosities, and that the fastidiousness of some might, in their imitators, develop into superfluous finicalities. Does not the presence of spirits like Schmitt or Sévérac, were there no others, prove that our music is also capable of strength ?

After having succumbed to the excess of Wagnerian ponderosity, assuredly we must not reduce our music to no more than an *article de Paris* ; but, truly, a school that is capable of giving us *La Mer*, the *Rapsodie Espagnole*, the *Poème de la Forêt*, and the *XLVIth Psalm* is not a manufactory of " sonorous *bric-à-brac*."

In this campaign against sonorous curiosities and *bric-à-brac* it is Maurice Ravel who has been the most frequently attacked.

It is on him that the peevish spirits, offspring of those who formerly vilified Debussy, visit the sins of musical France.   Though we thought it exquisite, *L'Heure Espagnole* cannot constitute a date in the history of French music, as was the case with *Pelléas*, but this amusing work, conceived in a profoundly French spirit, by a musician of extremely marked individuality, merits more attention, and is more suggestive of side-issues than some heavy symphonies or some too-well-written quartets.

Certainly a supple, precious, witty, and undulating mind like that of Maurice Ravel cannot be successfully imitated.   Just as in literature those who copy the stamp of Jules Laforgue will never attain to his cultivated spontaneity, imitators of the composer of the *Miroirs* and the *Rapsodie Espagnole* will only incur the risk of arriving at tricks that are less fascinating and of less value than his, for lack of a naturally complex sensibility to sustain them.

There is in present-day music no composer in whom are blended with better results certain attitudes of the mind that are at once irreverent and charming, sensitive and inconsiderate, and that delicately indicate the aversion from romanticism which is the most constant feature in the true sensibility of modern art.

The aspect of our race is discernible in this mirror. The clear-cut traits of which it is composed are reflected in its flowing water, animated by a vivacity that combines our most intimate predilections in subtle play. If one is slow to discover this, one must not be surprised. A like fate is the lot of all who perpetuate under our very eyes the qualities of our past.

When the *Histoires Naturelles* appeared, the pundits set up a cry of sacrilege. Then, tired of shouting or hissing, they denounced them with contempt as a joke. Well, let us have more jokes! We have been bored—no other word will serve— long enough by mighty contraptions. Often enough has the stock scenery of the *Tetralogy* been re- furbished for our benefit. So much the worse for the pundits! They are robust and numerous enough to defend themselves, and there will always be too many of them. One of the merits of the younger French School, one of its most constant aspirations, and the spirit that best establishes its French character, is precisely this cult of clearness combined with the fear of boredom. The works of

Debussy, Ravel, Roger-Ducasse, Roussel, Séverac, and others are clear and take good care not to be tedious. They contain nothing heavy or pedantic. They are not preoccupied with making serious music at all costs. They make music in accordance with their temperaments and their tastes. They have the advantage to possess temperament and taste. Whatever their music may be associated with, it will always be music in which one can take pleasure.

Careless of the respect due to the hierarchy of styles, Maurice Ravel came to think that, even for a musician who knows his business, lyric drama was not necessarily the only purpose of the theatre, and that the amusing aspect of things, of situations and of characters, could furnish adequate musical material, with renewed and attractive occasions to prove itself.

We have, as it happens, in France, an establishment subsidised by the State which bears the obsolete, but perhaps ironical, name of Opéra-Comique. Recent works performed there, be they *Manon* or *Werther*, *Aphrodite* or *Madam Butterfly*, *Louise* or *Pelléas et Mélisande*, conclude in the manner of drama without the comic element being, in fact, associated with them for a moment.

The opinion has long prevailed among musicians that *opéra-comique* is a negligible species. It is not certain that the opinion does not still persist with most of them, and the absence of modern examples would certainly lend colour to it. Before decreeing that *opéra-comique* was a negligible species, worn through to the last thread, incompatible with high-class music, it would perhaps have been as well to attempt it. The attempt would have had the result of proving, first of all, how many qualities need to be shown in it, and that it is perhaps easier to write a passably tedious opera than an amusing *opéra-comique*.

It is not that no one thought of it. We have had in France a man who would have been able to give new life to *opéra-comique* had he met with more support, had he not appeared at a time when gravity was more indispensable than ever, and had he further had the good fortune to discover a libretto worthy of him. That was Emmanuel Chabrier. With the libretto (oh, how badly written, and often ridiculous without being comic !) of *Le Roi malgré lui* Chabrier nevertheless succeeded in writing numbers that have survived and have nearly retained their first fresh-ness. They were experiments destined to have no sequel, and in which, owing to the libretto, were perpetuated decaying traces of ancient forms of *opéra-comique*, in which we can take no more pleasure.

And yet a good *opéra-comique* runs no more risk of becoming out-of-date than a good, or a passable, opera. All in all, *The Barber of Seville* remains more fresh than *Les Huguenots*, and *The Marriage of Figaro* more fragrant than *William Tell*.

It is not a question of reviving the forms of *opéra-comique* such as we should find them in Rameau's *Platée*, Dalayrac's *l'Eclipse*, or Mon-signy's *Le Deserteur*. It is a question of applying

to *opéra-comique* form the same ingenuity and the
same comprehension of the actual requirements as
were applied by Wagner in writing *Tristan*, or
Debussy in composing *Pelléas*.

It is against the view that such a task is unworthy
of a musician that we must protest, and precisely in
L'Heure Espagnole is its proof. And yet *L'Heure
Espagnole*, with its limited dimensions, and its *buffo*
character, does not solve the problem. It only
proves that in this direction a musician can do work
as useful in the artistic sense as when writing a
symphonic poem, or a quartet. What this new
form may be called, whether it be called " musical
comedy," is of little consequence. But that the
combination of literary and musical elements be
effected with more ingenuity and more subtlety,
that, it appears to me, is of unquestionable importance. In what proportion ? That is for the
musician's own genius to decide. Desire alone will
not write an *opéra-comique* or a musical comedy.
But it seems that our period in art is sufficiently
nourished with irony and culture, independence, and
aloofness from obligatory gravity, to adapt itself to
a less tragic form of musical composition in the
theatre.

Much would already be accomplished if one were
to be good enough to cultivate the habit of not
regarding that path as too insignificant for the
broad steps of musical dramatists.

It is from this point of view that Maurice Ravel is
to be congratulated. Those who did not wait until
the *opéra-comique* made up its mind to perform

L'Heure Espagnole before learning to appreciate the spirit and the quality of its music are aware that the merit of the work in itself justifies satisfaction a thousandfold.

Maurice Ravel has found here material to give a full rein to his sense of the comic, and of amusing and refined exaggeration. In this work are found again, but extended, the vocal methods that made the fortunate and merited success of the *Histoires Naturelles*. The contrast of characters is carried out with rare sureness. The part of Gonzalve is, in its entirety, one of the best examples of musical caricature that has succeeded in remaining delicate and truly musical. Those of Ramiro and of Concepcion suggest how much Maurice Ravel could accomplish for the stage if he were to devote himself to a work of greater development.

But what transpires above all from this *L'Heure Espagnole*, besides the vivacious personality of the composer, is the delicacy and tact with which he has contrived to avoid the insipid flavour of operette and the heavy humour of *opéra-bouffe*.

Equally distant from vulgarity and from bombast, this musical comedy pursues its course with spirit, combined with the twofold pleasant charm of a piquant vocal substance, and of the subtly coloured orchestration with which the *Rapsodie* had made us acquainted, and of which *Daphnis et Chloe* was afterwards to furnish the most exquisite of proofs.

The lack of eagerness displayed in mounting this work of a composer, of whom some disapprove, but whose rare worth none will dare to deny, is certainly not encouraging. The difficulty of performing a work which does not suffice to fill a programme, and which requires great accomplishments in singers and orchestra, and the impossibility of translating Franc-Nohain's libretto into a foreign language without robbing it of most of its flavour, combine to make *L'Heure Espagnole* assured, if one may say so, of no more than a restricted career. The importance of works of art is not indicated so much by the frequency of our contact with them as by the reflections they suggest.

At a time when true musicians are more than ever nourished on literature, when literature and music in France permeate each other more intimately than ever before, is one not in a better position than at any other period to produce musical works that will be to the lyric drama what *Les Plaideurs* or *Le Barbier de Seville* continue to be to the literary stage? Of course we do not demand that all composers shall proceed to produce a musical comedy for an exercise, as twenty years ago it was necessary to produce a drama with armour and Valkyries in it. We do not demand that works sent from the *Villa Médici* shall take the form of an operetta instead of a mass. But it seems to us that there are at present in France young composers whose nature is sufficiently acute and amusing, whose taste for irony and humour is sufficiently lively to enable them to endow music with new and charming sound-pictures. Is there not Sévérac? Is there not Roger-Ducasse? Is there not Caplet? Are there not many others?

Assuredly the thorny question will continue to be that of the libretto, for, if it is possible to write a good opera on a bad libretto, the feat is impossible where a musical comedy is concerned. But, if a wide search be made, according to the personalities of the composers and in accordance with their indications, it will be possible to find, among the comic treasures of humanity, themes of inspiration that will prove favourable to their vivacious spirit. These are only so many hypotheses and reflections suggested by a perusal of *L'Heure Espagnole*, and by an acquaintance with the minds of some of the young composers we love, and by the thought of the past of French music. Whatever foundation and justification they may possess, *L'Heure Espagnole* proves to-day that the comic sense and the musical sense are not so remote from each other as certain Puritans of music would have us believe.

ALBERT ROUSSEL'S *EVOCATIONS*

WHEN, on board the gunboat *Le Styx*, long ago, mid-shipman Albert Roussel watched the coming of the dawn on the banks of some Oriental and sacred river, within his sensitive and musical soul he was perhaps already dreaming confusedly of these *Evocations* of to-day. Perhaps in these *Evocations* there linger, revived by a recent journey in Asia, some of the impressions of that young naval officer of the past. Between those older impressions and their recent realisation lies a noble and serious life, and works of purity and beauty, fragrant with French charm and revealing a French soul.

It is not easy to know in what terms to speak of Albert Roussel. Those that one might use seem so much too blatant to attune themselves to a mind that delights in a discretion and a delicacy surpassed by none in these days. His work is created in his own image. It reflects him as the most faithful mirror, with his love of life without loudness, his restrained but lively ardour, his exquisite sense of pleasure, a thousand refinements without affectation, and, beneath this delicacy and this smiling nature, a gentle and firm power, with occasional melancholy.

With a slow sureness, over whose anxieties and hesitations he drew a jealous veil, he realised himself without stir, without attempting to attract anyone's curiosity, relying solely on his works.

To him came gradually those who collected the manifestations of the younger French music, and here they found some of the purest. They have loved his *Trio*, and the *Sonata*, which is the most alluring and the most ardent of our modern sonatas for piano and violin. When gathered together, or when alone, we have had sung to us again and again these songs, some ten in number, each of which lives again with more perfect charm at every fresh experience. Delights of the *Odelette* and the *Nuit d'Automne*, voluptuousness of the *Jardin Mouillé*, unassuming drama of melancholy farewells; which of us, in seven or eight years, has ever tired of hearing and rehearing them ? *Le Poème de la Forêt* voiced for us the soul enamoured of landscape that had already manifested itself in the three pieces *Rustiques*, and the sense of the picturesque that the form of a trio or a sonata contrived not to efface, and which thus renovated dogmas that are often too austere. When one follows the development of all these musical works, it seems as if one's mind were broadened by measuring their horizon, that widens from day to day. The view reveals, little by little, a more spacious domain, without taking one by surprise, but by imperceptible progress.

There is no composer who speaks less of his works than Albert Roussel, and there are no works behind which their composer effaces himself more completely than these. Yet they express themselves as much one way as the other, by discreet self-revelations and efficacious reticences.

In the *Evocations*, the same purpose has led him to tell his impressions regardless of theses, of ethnographic references, of geographical descriptions, and of all the apparatus that, in order to suggest authenticity, causes even truth to crumble and vanish from the heart. In his vision, dreams play as much part as realities. If his impressions were inspired by India, the country remains, at least in these *Evocations*, voluntarily undefined. Whether India, Tibet, Indo-China, or China, is of little consequence. Only the quality of the dream is to be considered, and that of Albert Roussel is suave and voluptuous. Darkness gradually disperses, in the distance appears the rosy City, which then fades away as in a mirage or a dream, and the choirs on the

banks of the sacred river see night dissolve at the
light touch of the sun, whom their united voices
greet with love.

The painter and the poet, who are present in this
musician from his earliest compositions, have been
able to combine with renewed strength in this work.
But, however Oriental or Hindu may be the purport
of such a dream in sound, the same ardour, the same
inborn elegance, and the same delicate sensuousness
are revealed in it as those which, in his preceding
works, made known to us in Albert Roussel one of
the most truly French souls of to-day.

The *Evocations* have been decisive in placing their
author in the foremost rank. Not for a long time
had so pure a work been heard, and it was a profound
joy to see manifested in this musical triptych all the
hopes that we had based upon a mind that knows
how to combine with a sure skill the more rare
qualities of communicative emotion.

The work's three sections: *Les Dieux dans
l'ombre des cavernes*, *La Ville rose*, and *Aux bords du
fleuve sacré*, follow, with inimitable sureness and
discretion, a combined plan whose contrasts only
strengthen its balance, and which concludes, without
undue emphasis, in the peroration, with a choral
symphony in which the voices are handled with a
precision so skilful that it is unsuspected.

Its ingenious orchestration nowhere reveals the
obstinate desire to attract attention that has too
often lessened the merit of modern works. The
employment of the instruments is governed by no
desire to master a theorem, but, more justifiably, by

I

the play of their colours and nuances, for the awakening of the imagination or the feelings of the listener. From the outset one is not confronted with an extravagant method. One thinks only of the pleasure of listening and being charmed, and of feeling at the same time all that such charm contains of rare and delightfully human elements. A sensation of completeness fills the mind with a satisfaction that is prolonged. One feels everywhere that grace and strength are combined without ever contradicting or colliding with each other. That is the merit of these supple architectures, which are durable and, as it were, relieved of part of their weight, and in which the mind that is penetrated with the voluptuousness of the earth is already steeped in an aerial longing.

Albert Roussel's *Evocations* are one of the seven or eight symphonic works composed during twenty years which will ensure, for a long time to come, the future of French music.

IV
SKETCHES FOR PORTRAITS

EMMANUEL CHABRIER

(*To Edouard Risler*)

HE had all the gifts of the mind, and yet how im-
placably is fate against him, even after death !
Will not the bad luck, as Baudelaire says, that did
not cease to torment him in his lifetime, give way
before the affection we bear him, through his works ?
Of this much we really must be convinced : there is
no French musician to whom fate has been more
unjust. Laurels have fallen to him with insulting
parsimony. And yet who could claim to have been
more of a musician than this fat, exuberant, enthusiastic, jesting, deep-feeling man who bequeathed
to us *Gwendoline*, the *Bourrée fantasque* and the
Pièces pittoresques, as well as songs whose pleasant
musicality has not been surpassed ?

So much unconstraint sometimes offends the taste
of the over-refined, but these fastidious people can
have had no inkling of the warmth and generosity of
his heart, animated by a many-shaded charm, which
is everywhere revealed in his music. At first one
finds it pleasant to follow this music. It has an air
of mirth ; a frank, and somewhat boisterous, manner
of presenting itself. There are some who stop at
that and say, " How funny ! " as they might of some
artist's prank, and they seek no further. And yet—
he is a man who endeavours to conceal his heart

with a laugh, who loves life, and finds in it a manifold enjoyment.

What do most of them know of him ?   It is much if their knowledge extends beyond inaccurate transcriptions of his works.

Who can hear the duet from *Gwendoline* without thrilling with pleasure, and what soulful merit there must be in the *Ode à la Musique* for it to relegate to the background a text of such unfortunate quality !

How many arguments have there not been advanced to cover him with oblivion ?   There are musical writers, not learned in the matter of dates, who reproached him with having commenced too late to compose : there are so many who begin too soon, and do naught else all their lives.   Others there are who, on the strength of a memory of *España*, distorted by some commonplace Wald-teufel, smile with indulgent pity when his name is cited.   There are even some who say that he is tedious, for it is really necessary that all be said, by Bouvard, and by Pécuchet.

Even Lalo, in spite of *Le Roi d'Ys*, has failed to receive all the recognition that is his due; but Chabrier does not yet receive the quarter of that to which his merits entitle him.   It is high time that we become convinced of this, and that we no longer perpetuate an injustice for which we ought to blush.

He had all the French virtues : good-humour, vivid sensibility, the sense of charm without affectation, and an inclination to tenderness that is interrupted by wit, only in order the better to proceed.   There is thus nothing that he fails to elevate, even when at first vulgarity appeared in prospect. He is often on the borderline of vulgarity, but he never crosses it. If he approaches the vulgar it is only in order to raise it, for he has health in grace, and sureness in joy.

Entrusted to the hands of another, his subjects would have yielded nothing but the commonest accents. See how the theme of the clarinets in the *Joyeuse Marche*, with its quaintly awkward gait, insensibly begins to tease the listener, and then dissolves in a smile, to reappear with grace. He loves to puzzle our ears. They think they know whither they are being led, for the paths are well trodden, but an unexpected accident intervenes, an accident that contains no risk beyond that of giving pleasure. At the other end of his domain he draws out, nearly to a drawing-room ballad, the languor of a sentimental motif; the line waves along and one expects the heart-rending eloquence of love-music for homely company. But a nervous movement insinuates itself, a nervous tremor slips in, and the melodic line is inflected into true tenderness. At the very heart of the *Bourrée fantasque* there passes with a sudden tremor an adorable emotion. He does not desire that it should linger unduly. Others would have caused the themes to exhaust themselves in frenzied passion and shamelessly display the excitement of *rubato*.

Such cheap scent is not to his liking. His music is redolent of fresh grass and hay, and of the joy of fine fruit that is proud of its golden pulp and its juicy flesh. He embraces it like a healthy girl of buxom figure, and whispers in its ear some amusing phrase that tickles it and imbues it with the freshness of real sensuous laughter. He loves the unambiguous sensuality that it exhales. And the time comes also when it takes his arm, perturbed as a maiden and tender as a poor human heart steeped in silence, in sweet echoes and in memories of love.

Are we then so wealthy that we can afford to treat with such neglect these ten *Pièces pittoresques*, with the exception of the *scherzo-valse*, that some find pleasure in distorting ? The *Idylle* and the *Mélancolie* are worthy of the most noble hands. As for the *Improvisation*, there is not, perhaps, in the whole of the French literature of the piano, a page of finer swing, of more delightful, or richer, form. We, to whom his pianistic performance is a legend, known only through the memories of the actual listeners, we can find its stamp on his pianistic style. He has impressed it on everything he has touched.

Le Roi malgré lui lacks nothing but a libretto worthy of the music. Why did he not persevere in this path of musical comedy instead of following the Munich road all the way to Bayreuth ? He could have given us that for which we are still waiting : a theatrical work that would be what *The Marriage of Figaro* is for Vienna and *The Barber of Seville* for Italy.

He had every requisite for it : a sense of true life, a genius for comic music that none has surpassed, unremitting fancy in the handling of the orchestra, overflowing imagination, and, above all these, a taste that remained surest in his most ardent mirth.

We measure our regrets by what he might have done, but let us give, to what he did, the affectionate melancholy of our dethroned joy. Is it possible that he is dead, who generously fashioned for us the *Cigales*, the *Petits Canards*, the *Cochons Roses*, the *Gros Dindons*, a diminutive Noah's ark, jovial and mocking, sailing towards *L'Ile Heureuse*?

Who in the domain of tones possessed, as he did, the abundant quality of true French gaiety? Ah! let us not suffer it to be lost. Above all, let us not disdain it in favour of accents that are more grave, and are often only the sinister voice of the dead who could find nothing to cherish.

Eternal joy of hearts, and of these French hearts, surpassed by none other because they are able to love suffering without caring to show it, and because they sing their tenderness under their breath in a smile!

VINCENT D'INDY

(*To Octave Maus*)

DIGNITY become music. The pursuit of a dream whose melancholy is enhanced by the feeling of being out of its own environment, and which carries within itself the regret of so many silent ancestors, of so many racial memories, and of mysterious words comprehensible only to his own advertence. A homesick aristocrat without disdain, he deplores the present time, is surprised that it should be his own, and pursues his work with faith.

Intimately bound to his forefathers and to his native Cévennes, the respect of traditions established itself in strength only to enable his mere existence to prove the vanity of tradition according to academic dogma.

No official sanction attended the first efforts of this tenacity of purpose. None would have enhanced its nobility.

The roots of this mind go far beyond the Italianism of the Conservatoires. Of what use would so futile a tutor have been to such an oak ?

A certain ruggedness of character, a hunger for solidity first drew him towards German culture, as much in literature as in music. It was an injustice at the time to observe in this only imitation or bondage. It was an essential sympathy, a search for equivalency. In this unconscious deviation, the logic of attraction was in operation.

It was Uhland who furnished the subject of his symphonic legend of *La Forêt enchantée* (1878). From Schiller he borrowed in turn the theme of his two symphonic poems : *Wallenstein* (1880), and *Le Chant de la Cloche* (1886).

At the same time his inclination towards large orchestral masses, towards the power of the symphony and the concentration of the lyric drama, urged him quite naturally to the study of the reforming genius who was already the author of *Parsifal*; and, by an inevitable attraction, the obsession of the Bayreuth master made itself felt by this ardent and sombre mind, full at the same time of discipline and of revolt.

Even in his Christian beliefs, which have since remained unweakened, he found himself at ease in Wagner's music, and *Parsifal* contained at this time the young composer's mysticism, at once anxious and robust.

But the brain alone was at work, and the Wagnerian influence or attraction could not entirely satisfy a sensibility that was the more durable and acute for screening itself behind this desire for knowledge, this preoccupation with technique, this aspiration towards an original form to which he could attain only by becoming profoundly conscious of himself.

Perhaps these ardent, sombre souls, wholly animated by an inner fire and by violence exerted upon themselves, reveal themselves only in contact with gentleness.

At the approach of César Franck, the personal inspiration of Vincent d'Indy emerged entirely. Then the keen, pungent scent of his home in the Cévennes deeply impregnated with a strong emotion the noble succession of his compositions. It was much less an influence than a meeting face to face. The influence of César Franck affects in d'Indy not so much the writing in the works, as the moral atmosphere in which they live. It diverts the author of the *Chant de la Cloche* from the often indigestible and doubtful æsthetic theories of the Bayreuth master, in order to replunge him in the very sources of his least sentiments : the native soil, the ancestral influences which inevitably constitute the essentials of every personality.

César Franck was not concerned with impressing his mould upon soft wax that had no future destiny, but by the contagion of his serenity he delivered from their disturbing uncertainties the consciences that had rallied to him.

Henceforth the mind of the composer has found itself, and the *Symphonie sur un thème montagnard* proves his own recognition of his own antecedents and the undeniable indices of his personality, rooted in the rugged and massive Cévennes.

From that moment the home-sickness of this soul from the Cévennes will constitute his real and profound originality, as much in the warm and earnest *Trio*, in the two *Quartets*, as in the two *Sonatas*.

Thus the best of him was in himself. His labour in search of his own genius, in directing itself to his native country, revealed the soul which animated both.

Among his works, which are now numerous and diverse, comprising lyric dramas, quartets, symphonies, lyric poems, and sonatas, one is entitled to believe that these, especially, will endure : the pieces in which his mind, rooted in the country, has reconstituted the fresh impressions of his childhood and his youth, the time when he was still unaware of the demon of Bayreuth, the time, perhaps, when he was not yet dreaming of composing music—the numerous pages in which are revealed that sense of the picturesque which is not in Wagner, and whose eloquence the skill of the author of *Fervaal* can only enhance.

His nostalgia is rugged and melancholy, but proud

and dignified. In his music it raises itself, with soul refreshed, above our consolations, which it does not invite.

Yet he does not disdain action, and does not shut himself up in his concern with a past that is forever abolished. Action always arouses him, and his taste for lyric drama is but one form of such incitement. He alone of the Franckist generation had truly the love of the theatre. It is in *Fervaal* and in *L'Étranger* that he succeeded in combining his Wagnerian sympathies with the affection he has for his native country.

Henri Duparc once said with some reason : " In France we have too great a love for dramatic music. Dramatic music is an extension and inferior species which does not allow the artist to express himself directly, to reveal freely the beautiful soul, the great soul that he ought to be, at the risk of being nothing."

Neither in *Fervaal* nor in *L'Étranger* has the dramatic nature of the music prevented d'Indy's strong character from expressing itself freely, and this robust and proud soul, sure of its skill, speaks there a moving language.

In his works, in his writings, in his sentiments is displayed a constant feeling of grandeur that puts fear into our contemporary meannesses wherever they encounter it.

When he is aroused to action, it is to defend or impose, not his own works, but those of the past which he considers the most worthy to put before the musicians of his day as models, and the modern works which are doubly dear to him for their own beauty, and for the ties which bound him to those who created them and are no more : César Franck, Castillon, Guillaume Lekeu, Ernest Chausson, Charles Bordes.

The meeting of Bordes and d'Indy was especially and necessarily to result in the creation of a permanent undertaking. The same ardour, more grave in the one, more passionate and more devouring in the other, gave birth to the *Schola Cantorum*. Among all the composers of their day there were perhaps no two whose minds inclined them more to devote themselves with such persistence to the defence of neglected or misunderstood works. So far as music is concerned, Charles Bordes was possessed by the demon of enterprise, and filled with apostolic fury and with a self-denial that, in disregard of all reason, restrained his interest in his own works in favour of those of his friends, of which he was the untiring advocate and champion. And Vincent d'Indy was animated with the same ardour, but more concentrated and tenacious, and concerned at the same time with the fame of his masters and with outlining the beauties of new works, even of those most remote from his own predilections.

Thus he will write in turn a standard work on César Franck, an ardent book on Beethoven, as readily as, on the morrow of the production of *Pelléas et Mélisande*, he wrote one of the most penetrating, accurate, and just articles upon Debussy and his tendencies.

Such application and such perspicacity are proof

of a high conscience. One may not appreciate all its expressions or all its features. One may even tolerate with regret this or that of its aspects. But it is impossible not to honour this proud, melancholy, and lofty mind.

The present is not always constituted to satisfy him, but his faith preserves for him an untroubled future. He does not disdain the time he lives in, but is a little remote from it, as if he pursued a dream, or distant memories amid which our presence gives him a sensation of incongruity. He is grave, as if feeling the weight of a moral solitude which is the heavier the more numerous the admirers by whom he is surrounded ; he maintains in his thoughts, in his reserves, and even in his kindliness, an obsession, as it were, whose nature one is not tempted to unravel, so innate does one feel it to be ; and in the music of to-day he is dignified and serene, with something in and about him that is somewhat like an exiled monarch.

Of this gravity and this vigorous conscience is born an authority that is, as it were, involuntary, and the more assured.

In this intellect there is a feeling of command. There are none in whom he does not command at least respect.

ERNEST CHAUSSON

(*To Camille Mauclair*)

A SOUL from the Round Table, from the time of elves, of water-fays, of rides through legendary forests, of love-lays and of attachments devoid of pretence, sustained upon ardour and respect. It is not by accident that Ernest Chausson made *Le Roi Arthus* the subject of his only theatrical work. That was exactly the atmosphere in which he was most at ease, and which one may find in many pages of his music. All that *Le Roi Arthus* needed is to have been born a little later, when emancipation was really beginning and when, breaking its Wagnerian shackles, musical art took the paths that, in the theatre, were to lead it to *Pelléas et Mélisande*, to *Ariane et Barbe Bleue*, and to *Pénélope*.

All that Ernest Chausson needed was to have less humility, less respect for masters who were lacking in the qualities which he possessed. Even in the little suite for *The Tempest*, composed, at the outset of his career, for a puppet-theatre, it is surprising how marked is the fluid and moving originality that was to display itself to better advantage afterwards, in the *Quartet*, the *Poème* for violin, in the *Concerto*, and in twenty lyrics that will long be remembered among the pages of the immortal album of the French song at the dawn of this century.

It is impossible to avoid remarking in Chausson's music the influence of César Franck. The master of the *Béatitudes* included the young composer among his most beloved disciples. But if it is true that Ernest Chausson yields the first place to César Franck, at least in genius, he surpasses him in the attribute of taste.

In order of time, Ernest Chausson was the first of his generation, after Lalo, Fauré, and Chabrier, to give proof of the most fundamentally French qualities, and the one who felt the most deeply the support that literature and the graphic arts could furnish to music in the search of its national character.

Even before they were appreciated in the world of artists, Chausson found delight in Carrière and Besnard and even in Odilon Redon, the prodigious and admirable. In literature he knew Moréas and Maeterlinck, Mallarmé and Mauclair, at a time when many musicians gave every indication of the most restricted critical sense.

He had at his disposal every means of security, being possessed of taste, material independence, and a thousand interests in life. But his soul was at moments beset with scruples. He did not always dare to be entirely himself. When one penetrates somewhat deeply into his music, and into the soul of which it still gives the reflection, one can come into contact with the bitter struggle of a mind that does not believe sufficiently in itself, and that still desires to be given its directions by others, when he could have relied for them solely upon himself.

Where he is himself, Chausson is nearly un-equalled. Others have more charm, more power, more refinement ; others succeed better in investing our minds by all the avenues of our curiosity, but none has greater purity than he, not even Charles Bordes, who was often exquisite, and whose nature was so fresh. Chausson's scrupulous soul is in-capable of evasion. At every moment we see it face to face in its entirety. It is only out of modesty that sometimes one of its aspects veils itself in

K

shadow. Though nourished, as he was, upon the literature and the painting of his day, this musician has the secret of youthful ingenuousness. His music has patches of white, as of a peaceful dawn rising upon the fairy ring in the forest of charm and enchantment.

Where he is himself, his emotion is pure and noble, with nothing to make us feel that it claims to outrange us. On the contrary, it is there, at our side, in a discreet attitude, waiting gently meditative for us to pay attention to the simple, lasting words it utters. Beside certain songs like *La Chanson Perpetuelle*, *Le Temps des Lilas*, and especially *Les Heures*, which count to-day with justice many faithful admirers, there are others by Chausson which deserve to be more freely enjoyed than appears to be the case. Such are *L'Aveu*, *Dans la forêt du Charme*, *Le Cantique à l'Épouse*, *Apaisement*, *Nocturne*, and *Le Colibri*. Chausson's soul is revealed in them, diverse in its constant purity, passing from juvenile and serious freshness to the melancholy to which his natural mood was more conducive.

But even his melancholy has no moments of excessive insistence. None has appreciated better than he the sense of discreet proportions.

Where he is himself, one can only cherish him ; and even when he is not himself, as in the symphony, where the figures of Wagner and of Franck are too closely indicated, he still succeeds in infusing a charm that is his only, and which makes bearable the avowal of such discernible influences.

He doubted himself a little too much, and the stupid accident of his death cut short his career whilst we were still hoping to derive from it so much personal and vivid emotion. He could have given to the French theatre a work of which *Le Roi Arthus*, in spite of its merits, was no more than a sketch, still entangled in the bushes of a past that is glorious but no longer serviceable to us.

This severance by a premature death, and the lamentable end of Chabrier, are the two gravest losses that French music has suffered in our time. But Ernest Chausson has bequeathed enough to preserve his name for a long time from oblivion, and to increase the number of his upholders.

In France, chamber music numbers few works of the quality of the *Quartet in A major*, and the *Concerto* for piano, violin, and string quartet. Together with Gabriel Fauré's *Quartet in C*, the first of these two works holds among piano quartets the same rank in the music of all periods as is held among string quartets by those of Claude Debussy and Maurice Ravel. In emotion the *andante* of Chausson's quartet does not even stand behind that of Debussy. The Franckist tendency of other works finds here, in this beautiful, full, and ardent phrase, a more serene sonority, and one of the warmest outpourings in the whole of modern music. And in the *Concerto* the whole personality of Chausson is unreservedly revealed, at once solid and delicate, serene and anxious, filling the classic frame and sometimes, happily, breaking its narrow restrictions with the effort of an eager, radiant heart.

His music is full of murmurs, of the swaying of branches, of fresh flowers suddenly scattered on his stealthy passage—full of freshness and of life, of nature, and of calls uttered through foliage whose shady density opens at times in the path of a warm ray. It is at once ingenuous and skilful music, and resembles the fairies, the water-fays, the elves, and Merlin the magician, expert in philtres and in the gathering of simples.

It is a path in the forest of legends, of lovers' rides, and of invincible vows. It is at once a new and a traditional avenue in the French forest.

HENRI DUPARC

(*To René Martineau*)

WHILST some are piling up symphonies upon lyric dramas, and quartets upon songs, there is a man to be met with whose work, famous for all time, is more or less limited to a book of a dozen songs. He seems to have taken the most jealous care to disclose nothing of his personality, and to restrict his work, at a time when it is the custom rather to make a noisy display of both. In spite of a fame that, spreading beyond strictly musical circles, has reached those in which music is a distraction, it remains none the less the fact that scarcely anything is known of his life. It is not easy to ascertain the date of his birth, or even his outward appearance.

There is, however, no need to dwell upon the exterior personality that clothes his mind, when our concern is to speak of his work. The most indiscreet curiosity would not reveal the mystery of a life of which solitude and silence are the incorruptible guardians.

All that is known is that he was a pupil of César Franck at the Vaugirard college, and that, long afterwards, he continued to find pleasure in associating with his master, who held him in particular affection. However, Henri Duparc was more the intellectual disciple than the pupil of César Franck. Of all those who followed the teaching or the advice of the composer of the *Béatitudes*, he is, perhaps, precisely the one who was least subject to his influence, and this despite the fact that César Franck influenced the minds of those who approached him all the more that his activities were devoid of all authoritative spirit, and wholly impregnated with kindliness.

The communicative faith of César Franck revived the beliefs of most of his disciples. One must set aside Paul Dukas, whom other hereditary influences endowed with an inquiring mind and a vivacity to which we owe the inimitable and delightful *L'Apprenti Sorcier*, far removed from Franckist ardour and aspirations. In Vincent d'Indy will be found again Franck's fervent spirit, sometimes a little strained, and always more austere. In the work of Chausson, whose line is sometimes inflected with a deeper melancholy, serenity frays a path through wavering anxiety; for, however strange such a coupling of terms may at first appear, it is possible to assert that the Franckist school is held together by an obsession of " serene anxiety " ; the aspiration of minds over-excited by the consciousness of earthly imperfections, and at the same time appeased by the certainty of a definite redemption.

The soul of the Franckist school is free from lassitude. In the master, the triumph of faith ; in d'Indy, Charles Bordes, or Guy Ropartz, the spirit of propaganda ; in Albéric Magnard a constant gravity ; in Ernest Chausson, an attraction towards all the arts and their new resources ; in all of them is a passion that animates and upholds them, leaving no loophole for discouragement to enter.

Lassitude is the soul of Henri Duparc's music. Comprised between lassitude of all movement, *Repose, O Phidylé*, and the desire for other countries that is inspired by the tediousness of all sojourn, *Invitation au Voyage*, Henri Duparc's music reveals almost continually a penetrating nostalgia whose theme is renewed by minute movements.

There is perhaps no expression more apt to throw light on the nature of Henri Duparc's work than the sentence in which Baudelaire says : " I have found the definition of the beautiful, of that which, to me, is beauty ; it is something ardent and sad, something a little vague, leaving scope for conjecture."

For Henri Duparc, beauty is of the same nature.

It is something ardent and sad, but this ardour is not set free, this sadness is not spoken, but is exhaled with poignant simplicity.

The art of these works is not complex, although the substance of the musical dream contained in them is rich. This art is not complex if the writing is considered in general. From the first moment, a line is revealed that is noble and of wholly classical purity. It is not until afterwards that we are struck with the delicate undulations of this line, in which is discovered a power of expression that cannot be surpassed by methods of refinement.

For example, the slowly swinging opening of the *Invitation au Voyage*, where two bars alternating, varied only by a semitone, depict an atmosphere of lassitude and of sweetness, until the moment when the idea of a possible " elsewhere " (*d'aller là-bas vivre ensemble*) is expressed by liberating the accompaniment from its initial monotony, whilst continuing to maintain the inflections of the melodic phrase in an atmosphere of uncertainty. This is Baudelaire's " something a little vague," and it does not cease to be expressed by the accompaniment, which remains unchanged until the moment where the recitative, " *Là, tout n'est qu'ordre et beauté, luxe calme et volupté*," rests upon chords modulating by semitones and devoid of all ornament.

It is nearly always thus, by means of nuances, that Henri Duparc gives accents to his dreams. Nothing is further from romanticism and from verbal lyricism, but perhaps nothing is nearer to the modern soul, whose deepest anxieties are betrayed, outwardly, only by almost imperceptible waves.

Ordinarily, his songs commence in the same calm atmosphere. The opening of *Phidylé*, marked " slow and calm," its chords gently modulating whilst the vocal phrase evolves " softly and without nuances " round the initial B flat, which acquires

a delicate value, evanescent, as it were, on its final
return when it illustrates with precision the idea of
unseen springs.

It would be possible to multiply such examples :
the first phrase of *Extase* and the last of *Lamento*.
Devoid of artifice, this art thus attains to an amplitude that is scarcely met with in any other French
lied, for such vocal lyrics as Chausson's *Chanson
Perpétuelle* or d'Indy's *Lied Maritime* are great works,
of nobility and power, but conceived quite differently
from the point of view of the method of writing.

Lassitude is the soul of Henri Duparc's art, but it
is a special lassitude. Rather would one call it
nostalgia. In it the soul neither complains nor
revolts, but plunges entirely into the dark waters of
spleen, which reflect the mirages of unattainable
" elsewheres."

Not even Debussy, in his marvellous *Cinq Poèmes*,
has understood better than Duparc to interpret
the soul of Baudelaire. It is with the same
soul that he has interpreted in music the nostalgic
words of the poet of *Fleurs du Mal*. It is the
same self-contained mode of expression, and the
almost unconscious evolution of thought ; the same
sense of imperceptible nuance, and the surprising
perspicacity of modulation in the inner life, expressed
by minute musical modulations.

Henri Duparc's choice of texts reveals his predilections : *Invitation au Voyage* or *Vie Antérieure*,
La Vague et la Cloche, *Extase*, *Lamento*, or *Testament*,
or even *Phidylé* ; poems of Baudelaire, Lahor, or
Leconte de Lisle ; it is nearly always a nostalgic

thought, a longing for rest, an obsession with lassitude or with death that attracts him.

Yet great romantic outpourings are not suited to his mind : as with Baudelaire, bitterness always maintains with him a constraint that forbids all transports, whilst the essential strength of character in both natures preserves them from effeminate and vain lamentations.

There is in Duparc's songs a modesty of expression and a discretion of accent which, in him alone, are associated with such constancy and such dignity. He says exactly what he wishes to say and travels no further, but he says sufficient to prompt the mind which is impressed by his utterance to further dreams of that " something a little vague that leaves scope for conjecture."

Why should the utterances of such a mind be so few ?   And yet those he has sent forth contain too many motives of emotions and of dreams for us to flatter ourselves that we can ever exhaust them.

PAUL DUKAS

(To Ildebrando Pizzetti)

ALL is exultation.   All is efflorescence.   The rapture of swift movement seizes upon all things.   All seems to be abandoned to its arbitrament, but suddenly each object falls into a place assigned to it by a secret will.   Behind each movement is revealed a serene control.   Chance plays no part in it.   At first, however, it seems as if the workings of chance were to be betrayed somewhere. At times one would think that disorder were going to spread; but soon all falls back into order, as if under the impetus of some mysterious power.

There is no more beautiful festival than that which is regulated in a manner at once assured, and yet discreet enough to impart an impression of complete liberty; to unchain the forces of joy, remaining able to restrain them at will, and to adapt them to a dominating design. An intimate struggle without violence. The sounds burst forth and subside as the water of a cascade that lets itself fall without respite, happy in its own play.

In the music of to-day there is no soul more enamoured of joy, but there is none better able to restrain itself. The evocations it suggests resolve themselves into silence at its will. Like the old magician in Goethe's ballad, " the master animates them only to make them serve his designs."

Yet no constraint is felt in them. Everything in them moves as by a natural play whose law is independence.

All Paul Dukas's music is animated by a constant desire of movement. The joy he pursues and attains is revealed as the unfolding, as the crowning of an efflorescence of effort. All in it confesses to an unquenchable thirst for rhythm, that derives satisfaction solely from itself. No music asserts more decisively the delight in movement. Immobility wearies it, and everything in it revolts against it.

Others are profoundly alive to the charm of

meditation and of indolent looking-on.   Dukas does
not remain satisfied with inaction.   One must prove
to oneself, by movement, that one is alive.

It is a marvellous spectacle, the intimate union of
this desire of expansion and this force of reserve.
The former gives to all his works the character and
the accent that makes them inimitable, whilst the
other makes him discover, with unfailing sureness,
the frames best suited to contain his thoughts.

It seems as if his choice of subjects were intended
to show, from the outset, the constant design that
guides him.   In this choice all betrays a hunger for
movement, as much the play of *Variations on a
theme by Rameau* as the *Apprenti Sorcier* with which
nothing can compare for the intensity of its mettle,
the impish vivacity of its accent, and the discreetly
comic spirit of its rhythms ; and again the adventure
of *Ariane et Barbe Bleue* in which is concentrated, in
legendary form, the struggle of the fulness and
boldness of life against the surrounding indolence.
This idea persistently haunts the composer's
thoughts.   It is as evident in his *sonata* as it is in
the *allegro spiritoso* of his beautiful *symphony*.

Yet the animation that directs them is not
feverish. Though modern, his music escapes the
unrest of our day.   There is none more serene, in
spite of its prodigious life.   His pages reveal themselves to us in all the splendour of their freshness,
and assume already in some places the assuaging
quality of the past.

There is no composer alive to-day who can
communicate to us in the same degree the impression

of a classic; and of all Paul Dukas's works the *Sonata in E flat* bears this stamp most deeply impressed upon it.

The power expressed in it is not out of proportion. It is not of the kind that lifts and carries one away beyond worlds, but it penetrates into us with confidence and communicates a lasting rapture, a reassured cheerfulness. It satisfies at once the demands of our thoughts and the vibrations of the senses, for the sagacious treatment of the themes, their permutations and their workings attest a constant affection for rhythm and all that it comprises of life-giving clearness.

Clearness and simplicity are the virtues of this mind. Its constant obsession with rhythm enumerates the complexities and necessarily reduces them. The study of each of his works shows the extent to which his will plays its part, and then one is surprised at having been so little struck with this at the outset.

In another so much will-power, such dominating preordination would entail a certain coldness. In him there is assuredly nothing of the sort. The ever-present emotion gives life to these constructions and ensures their survival. Already the *scherzo*, *L'Apprenti Sorcier*, has captivated the most diverse spirits and called forth everywhere unreserved approbation. Though less frequently heard, the other works present similar merits and deserve equal affection. Like all works that are rich in contents, they demand more time than most are prepared to give, in our too hasty day, to productions of the mind.

Despite its efflorescence of beautiful and engaging works, French music cannot offer many manifestations that, for nobility of the mind, rival those pages on which Paul Dukas has deeply impressed the coloured and vibrating reflections of his soul, which is fascinated with life, rhythm, strength, and joy.

What an impassionating sight, what an elating expression is the smile that denotes power !

ALBERT ROUSSEL

(*To Déodat de Sévérac*)

THE forest is bathed in mystery and in the light of a hesitating dawn. A gentle joy awakens among the trees, and roams at large ; and the summer mist, that still girdles the foliage with fleeting scarves, wraps in a harmonious silence the confidence of the dryads. And, as a sylvan ravisher of the smallest secrets of the nymphs, of their words of joy and of the raucous, burning cries of the fauns pursuing feminine forms, Albert Roussel evokes the amorous charm of imaginary bucolics.

It is not by a delicate subterfuge, or by some attitude of thought, nor for the sole purpose of musical description, that his mind has become attached to sylvan themes. His poet's soul inclines to spectacles in which reality and dreaming meet, where thought and the senses joyfully unite. It takes this direction whole-heartedly and with delicacy.

Concerned, in his visions, with atmosphere, he

evokes sometimes the real and vaporous landscapes of Corot. The colouring is, however, more brilliant in the musician. Albert Roussel's fauns have observed, on a suave afternoon, " upright and alone, under a modern flow of light," the faun of Claude Debussy.

It should occasion no surprise if one calls to mind painters, for preference, when speaking of Albert Roussel. The art of this musician is that of a landscape painter. He is absorbed in the desire to describe the aspects of a site, the rhythms it reveals, the light that plays on it, and its manifold murmurs.

Danse au bord de l'eau, Promenade sentimentale en forêt, Vendanges, Le Poème de la Forêt, Le Jardin Mouillé, Nuit d'Automne . . . it is an obsession with landscapes that is a feature of this soul, congenitally attracted to such sights. Thus the numerous hours spent formerly on the decks of ships seem to have left in him no traces deep enough to desire expression. The sea does not yet appear in his music, and there is nothing to give a presentiment of it whilst he is attracted by the capricious charm of nymphs.

Influences, sometimes contradictory, made themselves felt in his first expressions. His soul, divided between his varied ardours, and for a moment confused, hesitated, but disquietude was not his innate attitude, and his soul was only estranged by its surroundings.

Perhaps the deeper roots of his race did not come from French Flanders. Yet, on observing him, one is not surprised that he was born there. One does not easily escape from a set purpose to father the quality of his style upon the sensitive elegances of Watteau, the undulating line of Carpeaux, and the sweet, ardent, and weary charm of the poet who wrote the *Jardin de l'Infante*.

Again the same grace and the same smile, which in the musician is without lassitude or sadness. But at the very heart of this grace is the same French sensuousness. It is present in Watteau, in Carpeaux, in Samain, as it is here, this sensuous delicacy whose ardour no brutality comes to disturb. The abstract idea is not of their race. They do not understand beauty unless they feel it deeply, and enjoy it long. The universe is for them the inexhaustible sustenance of their fastidious avidity.

From his first utterances Albert Roussel is led by it. Since then he has applied himself to refining them at the same time that he was succeeding in making them firmer. Gradually the aspect of his thought betrays personal traits, captivating and harmonious.

He venerates the clearness and discretion of our race. His works have never ceased to bear its affecting stamp. Enamoured of literature and of nature, he establishes the equilibrium of a picturesqueness that fascinates the most fastidious, without there being in it anything intended to attract one especially.

He knows how to refresh his spirit at the sources of vegetal life. One dreams of those discreet ponds which reflect the beauty of the trees and a glimpse of the sky, and which, from the bosom of

their meditative beauty, bring forth, slowly to
germinate and blossom upon their surface, like a
desirable ecstasy, the unsullied calyces of water-
lilies.

At a time that is lacking in ingenuousness, he
prolongs the virtue of freshness and, without
effusion, opposes to the heavy burden of doctoral
theses the most acute taste for life. There is in it
neither trace of fever nor discouragement. Being
sensitive, he has not escaped experiencing the pain
of things, but he insists upon finding in it no more
than a new pretext for more fondly cherishing
them.

Yet there is nothing insipid. His songs remain
limpid, but succeed in avoiding banality. He does
not retire within himself in order to express himself
as ever the same. On the alert for new aspects, he
listens to murmurs ; he spies upon the unexpected
rhythms of groups that dance by ; he observes the
affecting curve of his universe, the new traits that
indicate its seasons, and, a sylvan enraptured with
his booty of pictures, he retires to some haven and
occupies himself in mating sonorities to express the
outlines and the very heart of his dream.

Its outlines are full of grace. Its heart is sensitive
and pure, and swells with voluptuous tenderness like
a bunch of fruit wrapped in the twilight of the first
autumn evenings.

He is loved, because, though skilled in his art, he
does not care to weight his works with science.
They are fruits which he has long surrounded with
every care, but he relies solely upon their intimate

charm, and the original savour that they communicate to those able to enjoy them.

He does not wish to disturb with cries and roars the woods inhabited by the dryads. The disputes of theorists do not seem desirable to him. He tarries, reads a poem, listens to a spring, observes a smiling nymph, sings of his dreams, and, like a dream, plunges into the heart of the forest.

FLORENT SCHMITT

(*To Gabriel Grovlez*)

FLORENT SCHMITT is one of the most important figures in French music of to-day. Not that he is considered as the leader of a school, on equality with Vincent d'Indy, Claude Debussy, or even Maurice Ravel. Florent Schmitt concerns himself little with schools, and his sensitive independence would not care for the bond of possessing disciples. He traverses French music of to-day like a wild boar of the Vosges, with the healthy robustness of a sensitive and crabbed nature, disdaining all coteries, dogmas, and ready-made religions or organised enthusiasms.

Born in Lorraine, he stands on the musical frontier of France and Germany. There is to be found in him that French refinement, that intellectual taste, mingled with rigorous preoccupations, and an appetite for greatness, that is not unconnected with Teutonic musical obsessions.

Florent Schmitt is a singular character in contemporary music. Whilst all are endeavouring to surpass their neighbours in originality, and often even sensibility runs the risk of being compromised to the sole advantage of singularity, he does not defend himself, in his works, from an addiction to forms reputed classical, although he is better acquainted than most with all the latest improvements in musical technique.

His *Quintet* is, in this respect, a highly characteristic work, at once classical and resolutely modern. He displays no more amenability to the past than to the future, but no less.

He submits to a strong discipline, but desires to accept it from none but himself, and therefore mingles, at his convenience, his recent predilections with the lessons of the past. He is a singular mixture of a passion for independence and an innate respect for rules. His choice tends wholly towards freedom, one might almost say towards anarchy ; and his nature inclines him towards submission to principles.

Florent Schmitt's originality lies in this rugged conflict fought with ardour.

From the teaching of the Conservatoire, where he reaped the supreme distinctions, he has succeeded in emancipating the quiet strength of his personality. No French composer of to-day, nor perhaps of any other day, can rival him in regard to strength, unless it be Berlioz.

The *XLVIth Psalm* and the *Quintet* are important works. The latter makes a vigorous pendant to Gabriel Fauré's delightful quintet, and these two works furnish sufficient proof of the variety of intonations the music of France can assume.

Florent Schmitt's genius remains always symphonic even in his songs, or in his *Musiques Intimes* for piano. However attractive his chamber works may be, it is not in them, the *Quintet* excepted, that resides the sphere of his emotional power.

At a period that comprises the quartets of Fauré, Chausson, Debussy and Ravel, the sonatas of Albert Roussel and Paul Dukas, and the trios of Vincent d'Indy and Maurice Ravel, Schmitt's quintet takes a preponderating place. It is one of the most important works in European music of the last forty years.

With Florent Schmitt, power is not accompanied by grandiloquence, and by this his critical mind reveals its French sources. In the *Psalm*, which is animated by a great inspiration and a devouring ardour, there is no room for rhetoric, nor for that hollow and bloated metaphysic which may satisfy more northerly races but which Latin genius cannot find to its liking.

The *Tragédie de Salome*, in its conception and in its realisation, is a manifestation of the complex art of Florent Schmitt, and of all that it contains at once of allurement and of violence, of ruggedness and of refinement, of solidity and of rich colour.

To those who would persist in believing, on the faith of ignorant reporters or relaxing melomaniacs that French music of to-day is no more than a game of subtleties, a musical toy-shop, Florent Schmitt's music is an excellent and fierce retort.

French music, like Shakespeare's drama, animates charming spirits, and others of more rugged character ; anxious minds and others possessed of greater assurance. It resembles the forest of the Ardennes, so propitious to legends ; it can be the sojourn of Ariel, who delights in the play of sunrays on the foliage, but it can also shelter the robust Ægypan who passes suddenly, like a harmonious storm-wind, carrying away with him, without seeming to be aware of it, our hearts and our minds.

MAURICE RAVEL

(*To Ricardo Viñes*)

HE is the *enfant terrible* of French music. His music puts everything on trial, asks indiscreet questions, manifests irreverent curiosities. It despises hierarchies and is concerned with nothing beyond being sincerely itself.

In his music life is a game that does not escape being sometimes overtaken by melancholy, but which an untiring ardour always preserves from tediousness. None has carried so far the pleasure of being fastidious whilst avoiding the danger of being insipid. Without noisy clamour it has succeeded in extending yet further the territory of tonal pleasure.

Everything in it conspires to provoke the longed-for emotions that are communicated by the spirit of *finesse*. This musical material, which is delightfully personal, regulates itself in an atmosphere wherein curiosity, irony, tenderness, sweetness, and even preciosity are always at home, and describe, without a false step, their spiritual arabesques.

Alborada del Gracioso is the title of one of the pieces in his set of *Miroirs*. Morning song (*Aubade*) of the *gracioso*—a word that defies translation, implying something like a buffoon full of *fineşse*, with mind always alert, and with irony ever in readiness : something like *Figaro*—Alborada, perpetually renewed, of a delightful *gracioso*.

For his ever alert mind it would seem as if night were never present, and for him it is ever the hour of the *aubade*, always the hour of smiles and of delicacy. He is skilled in pleasant mocking and is loath to vociferate. He enjoys the sweetness of living and is not unaware of its reflections. He dreams of charming memories and, long since, composed a *pavane* full of freshness, to the memory of a defunct Infanta, and its delicacy and *finesse* are such that the idea of death is screened behind them.

This early piece, as well as the two songs to epigrams of Marot, *D'Anne jouant de l'espinette* and *D'Anne qui me jecta de la neige*, revealed long ago Maurice Ravel's taste for delicately chiselled work, and a slight leaning to witty affectation.

Blame him who will ! Those are to blame who entrust to rancid songs the expression of their doubtful sensibilities and who, having encountered without effort the phrase adequate to tickle the coarsest epidermis, make it the everlasting theme of their output. Ravel is not a manufacturer of music, but an artist enamoured of forms and ideas. Instead of accepted ideas he prefers those which are rare, and the forms whose coloured arabesque charms the most fastidious minds.

It is impossible to deny that Ravel has an indefinable love of taking you by surprise, an inclination to hoax you with *finesse*, a love of curious shapes ; but it is not a matter of over-refined finicalities, of soulless efforts of patience on the model of the tiny ships that are constructed inside bottles,—bottles that are out of use and ships that never sailed. Ravel takes pleasure in contriving new and unexpected associations, in considering the elements of the universe in the aspect of expressive and sagacious deformations.

Most minds will never cease to regard the universe in accordance with absolute plans, and in hermetically-sealed compartments in which diverse sentiments, vices and virtues, ideas and forms, cannot mingle. And when there appears a mind concerned with thought and also concerned with preserving its thought from a thousand daily contacts ; one of the minds for which the idea is reality and strangeness is habit ; for which a smile is constantly a screen for the ardour of the heart ; then, the incomprehension of others is the fatal primary law, let those minds bear name, according to their period, Gérard de Nerval, Turner, Edgar Poe, Villiers de l'Isle-Adam, Mallarmé, or Jules Laforgue.

Perhaps some dramatic work will increase the number of the supporters of the composer of the *Miroirs*, as *Pelléas et Mélisande* did for Debussy ; but the most sincere of them were acquired from the time of the *Sonatine*, the *Miroirs*, and the *Histoires Naturelles*.

It is an exquisite and rare sensation that is imparted by musical works whose decorative line does not constitute their whole object, whose emotion is not their sole purpose, and whose principal attraction lies in concentrated allusions and unforeseen analogies.

These smiles conceal tenderness ; those unconstraints, ironic starts. None are so prone as mockers to be deeply moved, without indulging in excess and whilst preserving the necessary tact. These ironies disclose anxious tenderness and a certain modesty of the affections. Maurice Ravel is of the family of Henri Heine, Jules Laforgue, and André Gide.

But great is the indignation of those for whom gravity is the only rule and who proclaim that art is in danger the moment it has to do with smiling. Common humanity needs a certain quantity of avowed respect, and upsets itself if we seem not to be taking seriously that which, at bottom, it does not itself hold in respect.

This was seen when Maurice Ravel gave a hearing of the *Histoires Naturelles* at the Société Nationale.

The collection of little incisive pieces is well known which established the fame of Jules Renard. Drawn by a similar mood towards this ironic zoology, Maurice Ravel illustrated with a musical commentary five of these biting texts.

He did this with a suppleness of mind and form of which he alone is capable to-day, following, it is scarcely necessary to say, each text, word for word,

with a musical transcription in which imitative
elegance acquires a strangely broadened value ; but
reproducing the very atmosphere of these brief
tales, and creating around these descriptions, which
words necessarily restrict in spite of their power of
allusion, a broad and floating power of suggestion,
at once accurate and minute, of the landscape in
which these personages evolve ; and installing a
musical irony till then unsuspected.

It was a genuine scandal, and, in the eyes of some,
amounted almost to a crime of *lèse-majesté*. This
young composer was scarcely loved, but he was, however, taken seriously. He was considered uninteresting as a musician, but accepted in good society. And
here was he, by an intolerable frolic, offending
against the respect due to music itself, making the
art of Beethoven and Mozart serve for the expression
of boyish pranks. And the old, effete guardians of
the great principles veiled their faces, and, as it is
said in the Scriptures, every hair of their flesh stood
on end.

O eternal hatred of the doctors of the Temple for
the delightfully inconsiderate spirit, that, born of
cultured brains, preserves throughout the ages the
most admirable resources of our race ! O musico-
graphers crouching behind dusty texts, who, in
every age, endeavour to interdict, in the name of
your indigestible trash, the life that is unceasingly
renewed !

Perhaps the defence of the *Histoires Naturelles*
was sometimes undertaken with excessive ardour,
but this is excused by the exasperation that arises

at the contact with those who have awarded themselves the monopoly of all that is serious.

Despite whether one liked or disliked this kind of wit, there was in these five songs too much originality and too much skill for them to continue to be disparaged without the risk of ridicule. Apart from a few sectarians who remained fixed in their first attitude, word was then passed round to declare, with an air of dismissing the subject, that it was merely a jest.

Words are so supple that a mutual understanding depends upon the sense in which one understands them. Ravel's *Histoires Naturelles* may be a jest ; but then Laforgue's *Complaintes*, or André Gide's *Paludes* are also jests.

Jests, if you like, but jests which are not within the reach of the first comer. To handle this sort of thing requires sureness, precision, and minuteness of gesture, otherwise the exaggeration is betrayed and caricature debases what was undertaken by the finest intelligence.

Critics have been found to assert, with more insistence than good faith, the close musical relationship of Ravel with Claude Debussy, and to declare that the composer of *Miroirs* is a mere imitator of the master of the *Estampes*. Time is slowly dealing justice to this contemptible allegation.

The harmonic emancipations which were innovations by Debussy are to be found again in the technique of Ravel. The contrary would be inconceivable, and one can no more be surprised at it than at meeting their traces again in the works of

Albert Roussel and Florent Schmitt. At this time of day one cannot contrive that Claude Debussy never existed, and it would be somewhat ridiculous to endeavour, with conscious effort, to write without making use of the new resources brought to life by Debussy's art.

There is more in it than that. A renovation of such extent is not the achievement of one solitary will, even that of a genius like Debussy. It comes to existence by the operation of latent desires which accumulate and claim fulfilment. The influence of Claude Debussy is felt in certain works of Maurice Ravel (some will say in the *Miroirs*, and others in the *Quartet*); that much is certain. Maurice Ravel and all of his generation know and cannot forget what they owe to the composer of the *Images*, and the *Prélude à l'après-midi d'un Faune*. But it must not be forgotten that *Jeux d'eau* is, in point of date, one of the earliest manifestations of French pianistic art in our day, and that the *Pavane*, the *Quartet*, and the earliest songs, such as *Sainte*, had already given proof of the clearly original mind of Ravel, in whom concentrated emotion, a tenderness repressed in pleasantry, and an observant penetration, are steeped in the affectionate irony that is the basis of his views of the universe and the conclusion to which his introspection has led him. Perturbing and witty *gracioso* whose *alborada* leaves indifferent none who hear it ! One is left to choose only between finding it unbearably irritating or enjoying it, as I do, with others, more and more, as one of the most adorable victories of the modern musical spirit, as one of the expressions in which are concentrated the sense of observation and the sensibility that constitute the best part of our genius since the *fabliaux* and the early folk-songs ; since Villon and du Bellay ; since Marot and Michel de Montaigne.

(1907)

Ten years have passed since this sketch was published. Since then Maurice Ravel has given us in the *Rapsodie Espagnole*, in *Ma Mère l'Oie*, in *L'Heure Espagnole*, in *Daphnis et Chloé*, in *Trois Poèmes*, and in the *Trio*, new reasons to rejoice, and added new riches to French music. The views expressed in this sketch have been abundantly justified. I take special delight in having insisted, so far back as 1907, on the particular quality of sensibility and of sentiment in Ravel, at a time when he was denied all tenderness and only credited with ingenuity. The sentimental freshness of *Daphnis et Chloé* has only accentuated that which some of us anticipated from the *Pavane*, the *Sonatine*, and the *Oiseaux Tristes*.

DÉODAT DE SÉVÉRAC

(*To André Caplet*)

HIS is a strong and ardent soul, at once sensitive and robust, wholly possessed by a fire that smoulders and shows itself at moments in a pure flame, with which it gives a pervading light to his noble and affecting horizon.

This vigorous soul is, however, devoid of violence. It does not appear compelled to restrain itself. It shines with a serenity in which his joy finds control and his melancholy obtains firmness. Never is the expression of the thought surprised into excess, but never is it overtaken by mediocrity.

In music this man speaks seldom, and only when the movements of his meditations have led him to it. Thus he offers the astonishing spectacle of works that, wholly bound up with describing the exterior aspect of things, yet attain more surely than any others to the essence of human sensibility and emotion.

Two sets of piano pieces, *Le Chant de la Terre* and *En Languedoc*, and some ten songs, constitute at present all that has revealed this mind to musicians. They suffice to assert one of the strongest personalities of to-day and one of the most powerful among the writers who entrust to the piano the expression of their thoughts; not that he adapts himself to it with all the ease in the world, but because he surpasses it. Others know the minute subtleties of pianistic writing, and the embroideries of their style come to light in constantly varied patterns, and are refined away to vaporous trifles. His concern with his style is limited to enclosing the major power within the narrow space of a piano-poem, and it is from the fire that animates him that his musical utterance draws all its colour. It does not thrill so much as it penetrates you with everything that is exhaled by its aspects. Its charm derives not from arabesques or from rich contrasts, but from a broad and new simplicity.

The horizons described by these poems are not smiling or flowery, but they bear always the stamp of a secret gravity. Their lines are noble and simple. In them the earth is not constantly concealing itself under the pleasantness of the foliage. All in them reveals the fecundity and the virile frankness of life.

Ardently attached to his natal soil, he has understood it to the point of discovering the secret of vaster landscapes even than those which lay before him, and, whilst seeming to restrict himself to the depiction of the Languedoc landscape, he was in contact with the very essence of the French landscape wherever it is more grave than smiling and more noble than graceful. And, transcending even our national borders, he seems in *Les Moissons*, in *Sur l'Étang le Soir*, and in *Coin de Cimetière au Printemps*, to have attained to the gentle nobility of the earth itself.

Nature, broad and beautiful, sometimes rugged and sometimes sweet, is the domain that suits him. He has not ceased to live in it, making of it his ordinary residence or, when circumstances detained him at a distance, the habitual subject of his musings. His sojourns in towns have been short, and limited to the requirements of his musical studies or of his friendships. He is not at his ease in them, and soon returns to Saint-Félix-de-Caraman, where dwells his heart.

What virtue lies in a work in connection with which one can use, without insipidity, that word, so full of traps for the unwary : the heart ! I know of

ncthing to equal these pages full of serene and at
once ardent affection in this limpid atmosphere,
alive with vigour and grave joy—I know of
nothing to equal them but certain poems of Francis
Jammes, in the *Élegies*, particularly that which
commences :

Quand mon cœur sera mort d'aimer.

The same love of form at once dominates and
emancipates them. More minuteness in Jammes,
but in Sévérac more colour. An atmosphere
unceasingly renewed and favourable to their
thoughts enveloped their art-dreams, and, both
born in the midst of landscapes whose noble and
beautiful lines charmed their vision, they impart
to each page of their poems the aroma of healthy
life and of virile gentleness that cannot fail to
move us.

We must not carry this too far, and let a partial
analogy aspire to prove equivalence. The points of
resemblance of the poet and the musician are limited
to the matter of their rustic sensibility. Their
themes and their tastes diverge. They are different
flowers. The same atmosphere makes them to
bloom, and it is their roots that touch.

There is in Sévérac, as it were, a determination to
be healthy, and, even in melancholy, a robust
passion. Does not this title, *Coin de Cimetière au
Printemps* reveal his mind ?

This churchyard corner, this familiar corner, does
not prompt him to express tender lassitude. It is
not his intention to be definite, and in the graveyard

he sees living flowers. He hears arising the universal joy of effort that has not reached its summit. A *coin de cimetière*, but *au printemps* ; and over the rich and grave harmonies of the bass the freshness of living hopes is singing and asserting itself.

In every page of these works that which strikes one first and leaves a lasting impression is the feeling of fulness in the form. Nothing is displayed as an eventuality. All is achieved. The harmonies fertilise each other mutually and do not resolve until assured of complete maturity. It is the quality of those who do not speak unless under the stimulus of their fervour.

There exists, to describe this attitude of the mind, no word more adequate than " fervour."

Besides, it is the keystone of the arch of meditative criticism. It is the touchstone of minds which are not solely of to-day. No word is more noble or contains more of concentrated ardour or of radiant meditation.

" Nathanael, I will teach thee fervour," says André Gide, who knows fervour so well, at the opening of his *Nourritures Terrestres*. Sévérac also teaches it to us. He is a simple and strong picture of it. In it is seen to reign that passion of love that turns from blatant utterance. And behind the joyously or gravely smiling face is so fertile an *arrière-pensée* !

(1908)

ERIK SATIE

(*To W. G. Whittaker*)

1866.

AT Honfleur, where Eric Alfred Leslie Satie, known as Erik Satie, was born in 1855, one breathes of necessity, and by a decree of divine fate, a love of special and manifold phantasy, together with the inconstant breeze of the estuary and the beauty of one of the most affecting views in the world. The most vivid imagination and the most compact logic mingle there in variable proportion. An unforeseen chemical process is elaborated there and gives birth, according to the dose, to minds like Albert Sorel, Henri de Régnier, and Lucie Delarue-Mardrus, or else like Alphonse Allais and Erik Satie.

The contempt for beaten paths, the hunger for the unknown formerly led the mariners of Honfleur, of set purpose, to seek suspected Acadias [1] or mysterious Africas. In the music of to-day Erik Satie has given us its equivalent, perspicacious, imperturbable, and bantering.

Others are revolted, I am told, by our pausing over the works of Satie, our finding pleasure in them, and, even further, holding them in esteem. I am sorry for them, but Satie's smile and his indifference to superannuated dogmas have done music better service than much pedantic assurance. It is hazardous to conclude, from a man's capacity to smile, that what he says is only amusing and has, in truth, no importance. The work of Satie is modest.

[1] Acadia is the old French name for Nova Scotia.

It does not aspire to be grandiose. It readily consents to efface itself. It has long shared an impenetrable remoteness with its author, who has little inclination to confidences. His works waited nearly twenty-five years after their creation for Maurice Ravel to think of restoring them to the light they deserved, in order that Satie should be credited with the merit that is his due.

In the days when Erik, then eight years of age, was being initiated in the musical arcana under the direction of an organist of St. Catherine, a picturesque wooden church on the Honfleur coast, he surely had no thought of revolutionising music. Yet the familiarity with the plainsong to which his professor accustomed him impelled his naturally active mind to find pleasure in the most emancipated sonorous combinations, and to travel away from tonality.

At the Conservatoire his circumspect indolence led to his being sent down from a piano class. Afterwards he was a fellow-pupil with Chevillard, Paul Dukas, and Phillipp in the piano class taught by Mathias, and his professor advised him to go and study the violin, which was more likely to be of use to him. Disdaining such specious advice, Erik Satie attended a composition class as listener, but henceforth, although a listener, he gave constant preference to the more liberal teachings of medieval religious polyphony.

He was scarcely more than twenty years of age when he composed the *Sarabandes*, in 1887. It would be possible to date from then an entire

M

history of the French colour in music, for, by means of a conscious and wise disrespect of the principles of the Conservatoire, Erik Satie was inaugurating the musical methods towards which Claude Debussy was tending at the same time, and to which he was to give a personal stamp.

These early *Sarabandes* have recently been reconstituted, as well as the *Gymnopédies* which followed them. We are ravished to-day by their charm which formerly—and here formerly means only yesterday—caused stupefaction and gave scandal to some, and made others shrug their shoulders.

In order to discipline himself Erik Satie composed his pieces three times over, nearly in the same manner, but with subtle nuances. There are three *Sarabandes* and three *Gymnopédies*, just as there were later to be three *Gnossiennes*.

For self-justification and to test the measure of his success, his attempts are made in threes : " *les deux manches et la belle*," as their author says with a sly smile.

There have been some who believed that the intention to give surprise, the inclination to freedom, or the contempt of ordinary rules could alone have actuated Erik Satie when revolutionising the tonal idea without appearing to touch it. But, much to the contrary, his phantasy was directed by a strict application.

He imposed upon himself slow dance-forms : Spartan and sacred dances in the *Gymnopédies*, and dances of Pelasgic Greece in the *Gnossiennes*,

mingling minute refinements with the pleasure of
barbaric sensations. One cannot escape the charm
of the third *Sarabande* or the suave gravity of the
second ; and the form of pulsation that governs
the *Gymnopédies* is bathed in a delicate atmosphere
that has not tarnished its premonitory colouring.[1]
Nowadays the second *Gnossienne* might almost be
reproached with a too easy melody, but the barbaric
delicacy of the first has lost none of its accent.

When he wrote the *Gnossiennes*, in 1889, Erik
Satie had found two supports in his researches, or
rather two confirmations of their legitimateness :
the Javanese dances at the Exhibition of 1889, and,
more especially, the Greek choruses at Saint-Julien-
le-Pauvre. A little later, carried away by the
mystic symbolism that prevailed at the time, and
with which he was in sympathy, at least in his
obsession with plainsong, he composed the *Sonneries
de la Rose+Croix* (1891), and the *Prélude du Fils
des étoiles*, a *Wagnérie Kaldéenne* by Joséphin
Péladan, performed at Durand-Ruel's house in
February, 1892. With the *Prélude de la Porte
héroique du Ciel*, composed in 1894, they constituted, in the development of their author, the
second manner, in which the sentiment of mystic
purity is substituted for the more essentially
rhythmical direction of his earlier works.

It was about this time that, at the Auberge du
Clou, Avenue Trudaine, where he played the piano,
Erik Satie became intimate with a young musician

[1] M. Claude Debussy has orchestrated with consummate art
the First and Third *Gymnopédie*.

who was enamoured of new or revived sonorities, and who displayed curiosity about the author of the *Gymnopédies*. It was the composer of *The Blessed Damozel* and of *Cinq Poèmes*, then styled Claude-Achille Debussy.

It is not devoid of truth if one believes that the conversation of these two young men, diversely devoted to music, and Erik Satie's emancipatory studies in the question of tonality, contributed in some measure to the æsthetic of *Pelléas et Mélisande*. That alone would entitle Erik Satie to notice for the part he has played.

But, careless of obstacles, this fantastic and methodical musician, whose very existence remained unsuspected, was composing pieces in a style of greater freedom. Wholly saturated with a humility of which one can only assert that it is not assumed, he infused into his titles the sense of humour that was gradually to lead him on. Thus, as early as 1897, he completed the *Pièces Froides*, whose six numbers, three and three, according to his custom, are grouped under the modest sub-titles of *Airs à faire fuir*, and *Danses de travers*. Gradually the reins he had harnessed to his fancy were loosened, the *andantes* of the outset tended to be replaced by more rapid movements, and a smile came to give more animation to a too constrained gravity. These new views gave birth in 1903 to the *Morceaux en Forme de Poire*, whose titles earned for them a contemptuous attention, which was less than they deserved.

The sense of method which does not leave Satie and, in accordance with his Honfleur heredity, actually leads him to the varied domains of fancy, persuaded him to resume, when over forty years of age, the way of the schools. From the Schola Cantorum, which he attended, he derived the benefit of two scholastic sets of pieces, the *Aperçus désagréables* (Pastorale, Chorale, and Fugue), and *En habit de cheval* (Chorale, Litanic Fugue, another Chorale, and Paper Fugue), self-imposed tasks, respectfully written to prove to himself and to others that it is possible to write tedious works and yet to write them with a sense of humour.

Since 1912 the composer of the *Gymnopédies* has given us in succession : *Véritables préludes flasques (pour un chien)* ; *Descriptions automatiques* (April, 1913) ; *Embryons desséchés* (June, 1913) ; *Croquis et agaceries d'un gros bonhomme en bois* (July, 1913) ; *Chapitres tournés en tous sens* (August, 1913) ; *Vieux séquins, vieilles cuirasses* ; *Heures séculaires et instantanées* ; *Trois valses distinguées du Précieux dégoûté*; *Choses vues à droite et à gauche* (for violin), the last three works being as yet unpublished.

A productiveness so suddenly become abundant, on the part of a spirit diffident in itself, and almost in its audacity, would not be compatible with works of constant value, but their very abundance indicates a happy generosity in their vivacity.

With all due respect to those who may regard such inventions as useless, it is perhaps less difficult to write a symphony, such as there are several, devoid of true music, than to raise humoristic fancies above the mere style of the music-hall and impart to them a musical quality. It is Erik Satie's merit to have preserved in these amusing short sketches the evidence of a skill that does not attempt to impose upon itself.

The titles and the improbable indications of nuance with which this humorist ornaments his pieces (*Tyrolienne turque*; *Affolements granitiques*; *Fugues à tâtons* . . .) must not be allowed to make us lose sight of the musical quality of his works, which these literary elements would not suffice to sustain. Whether he engages in disconcerting adaptations of familiar themes, as in the *Tyrolienne turque, Españaña*,[1] *Celle qui parle trop*,[2] or *Sur un vaisseau*,[3] or derives a comic effect from the grotesquely expressive employment of serious means, as in the theme of the two horns in *De Podophtalma*,[4] he does not cease to be musical. In this respect the books of *Embryons desséchés* and of *Vieux séquins, vieilles cuirasses* remain affecting records of the happy meeting that may occur between music and the spirit of fantastic banter. In the second of these sets the first piece, *Chez le marchand d'or*, proves that Erik Satie knows how to write very effectively for the piano, just as *Seul à la maison* in the *Véritables préludes flasques* gives proof of an emotion which generally forces itself not to appear, but by which the composer sometimes allows himself, without regret, to be betrayed.

To have had the intuition of the harmonic revival

[1] From *Croquis et agaceries d'un gros bonhomme en bois.*
[2] From *Chapitres tournés en tous sens.*
[3] From *Descriptions Automatiques.*
[4] From *Embryons desséchés.*

to which the name of Claude Debussy will remain attached, to have succeeded in endowing French music with little works that are full of agreeable quality and will not age any sooner than do more pretentious pages: is that not enough for us to honour Erik Satie, to have some gratitude for him and to award him, in the music of to-day, the modest place that he does not claim, but that musicians like Debussy and Ravel have claimed on his behalf, and that only those minds that are burdened with relics, as in the fable, consider it unseemly to grant him?

V
MUSIC AND POETRY

BAUDELAIRE AND MUSIC

(*To André Gide*)

LET us tarry on the banks of an attractive and singular river that is impregnated with grandeur and melancholy. The waters of this river are bitter. Its banks are sombre and beautiful. An internal agitation animates its waters and clouds them. Strange flowers torn from its banks are carried down angry currents. None knows precisely where this river has its source. Its surface is at times rippled with a new tremor whose suddenness startles, astonishes for a moment, and then attracts.

Yet no fury assails its languid or rapid course. In places the water seems more limpid and reveals a marvellous efflorescence. It betrays furtive comings and goings which play in the light of an unforeseen and distant horizon that seems to be reflected, at unsuspected depths, into magic radiance.

Often the waters of this river are tinted with metallic reflections. Fallen leaves float upon them. Indolent and treacherous creeping plants suddenly intertwine. An acrid perfume reveals that its waters are tainted by decomposed fragments. Their tints are then unimaginable.

Sometimes again these tints contract, and the river seems like a tarnished mirror, concealing with difficulty sumptuous landscapes. And this river flows unceasingly on its royal course, with ardour, or languidly ; full of anxiety, or slowly, with an indolent serenity. And always over its triumphant and fateful course there reigns a misty atmosphere which sometimes thickens to the point of concealing from us its attractive curves.

Only now are the fogs beginning to lift with which this river voluntarily enveloped its sources and some of its aspects.

It is indeed only recently that the true light of day has begun to be shed upon the physiognomy of Charles Baudelaire. In the whole of French literary history there is none whose features have been distorted with less regard for truth. A legend clings tenaciously to the memory of this poet.

There are legends that surround memories with such halos that one regrets to probe them and prefers not to advance too far for fear of seeing the illusion one has preserved of them crumble away into acrid and colourless dust. There are other legends that one devotes oneself with some delight to destroy, whereby historic truth is posthumously avenged on the enthusiasm that makes reputations hurriedly and is not always sufficiently well informed to destroy them. The legend of Baudelaire is one of those that should be pierced, for, although it does not affect the poet's admirers, it does not avoid estranging from him, on the faith of perpetuated gossip, certain desirable affections, and it prevents one from appreciating the importance played by this writer at the end of the last century.

Yet one cannot bear any grudge against those who, whether through credulity, indolence, or animosity, actively continued to give a doubtful character to the destiny of his memory; for the one who was most active in this direction, and possessed the most authority and the most zeal, the one who constructed the most minutely this satanic, disturbing, and perverse legend of Baudelaire, was none other than Charles Baudelaire himself.

He has said somewhere: "Chaste as paper, sober as water, devout as a communicant, inoffensive as a victim, it would not displease me to pass for a profligate, a drunkard, a blasphemer, and an assassin."

He was born with a singular sensibility that was only exasperated by circumstances. These even appear to have been the most suited to irritate and impress his nerves, which, from childhood, were delicate, vibrating, and equally ready to relax and to contract.

One of his diaries, which he entitled with such accuracy "*Mon cœur mis à nu*," reveals him as he was in childhood. Minds such as that of Baudelaire are not shaped suddenly; their roots establish themselves slowly. There are some whom solitude attracts, as if in spite of themselves, and as if it were their native atmosphere. Their senses are sharpened to the point where every clash is to them a wound, and where the compassion, the curiosity or the authority of others can be, for them, no more than so many further reasons to withdraw into themselves.

It is not that they are from the first palled with what life offers them, but they need silence to enjoy it at leisure. Their nerves make them sensitive to everything, and the universe arouses their solicitude. Their aptitudes are numerous and their curiosities manifold. Their childhood is a succession of enthusiasms and meditations, of desires and lassitudes, without sufficient power of concentration to hold them at any point. Authority, which satisfies others, is necessarily unbearable to them; not that disorder is their law, but because they obey their own sense of order, whose origin lies behind that of law, at the roots of their very being. They maintain even in their excesses the measure of their dignity. They are obstinate and timid, peaceful, yet always in revolt. Their ordinary attitude is calm, but in their heart a disturbance is seething that they know not to whom to confide, and they exasperate themselves in the endeavour to find a responsive echo to it.

They keep within themselves melancholies that naught could appease, and throw themselves into agitation to dispel their obsession.

They are sensitive to the most minute accentuations of the instant that passes. They watch the modulations that vibrate around and within themselves. One can understand what the youth of such minds may have been, only when maturity has permitted them to express it with more precision.

Meanwhile, the love of silence in these reserved souls, and the irony with which they surround themselves, give a misleading impression of their qualities.

They are always animated by an unsatisfied tenderness that knows not how to express itself, in its fear of banal formality; and this fear leads them to studied refinement, and to the cult of the bizarre or the unexpected. Those who are enamoured of ordinary good sense, and of sentiments that find expression so soon as felt, cannot understand these taciturn children who are irritated by every question and who derive strength in the same degree as they do sadness from their irascible humour. All that they do is to ask silently of those who surround them to give them wise affection and undisturbed peace, that they may attempt to answer the questions that crowd within them, and to appease the tumult that has been let loose in their hearts by an impulse communicated from without, and that only death will interrupt.

Truly, the most regrettable event in the life of Baudelaire seems to have been that he lost his father at an early age. The misfortunes of his life were to be aggravated by the accidents that followed as consequences of that death.

Charles Baudelaire's father had been a tutor in the family of the Choiseul-Praslin, in the time of the Revolution. Under the Terror he was able to render numerous services to his friends. He was a distinguished spirit, full at once of *finesse* and of unassuming good nature. He was readily compared to La Fontaine for the simplicity and originality of his character.

Charles Baudelaire owed to him the love of writing, and the passion for elegance that he retained in the midst of vexations and difficulties. There is no doubt that he would have met with encouragement from his father in the inclinations that drew him to literature and had been the means, in M. Baudelaire senior, of ensuring refined associations and some social standing. But when his father died his mother was still quite a young woman, and at the end of a year she married Colonel Aupick, then in garrison at Lyons.

Baudelaire was destined to retain all his life the bitterness of this remarriage. At the outset he was little inclined to look upon his stepfather with a kindly eye, and it happened that that otherwise praiseworthy officer possessed precisely the character least suited to understand that of Baudelaire. This commanding officer, born with the love of action, could not understand the young man who was haunted with dreaming and curious of the least vibrations of a surprising sensibility, whilst preserving an appearance of impassiveness, irony, and enthusiasm : a mind shaped too early and gradually concentrating, to bloom afterwards in the unique work of genius that is *Les Fleurs du Mal.*

The journey which he was compelled, by his stepfather's authority, to make to Mauritius and India, left on his mind a most vivid impression. The sight, however brief, of these tropical horizons, of these countries with gorgeous vegetation, threw his already nostalgic soul into prolonged and violent excitement.

Unlike other poets who were born there, such as Leconte de Lisle, Lacaussade or Léon Dierx, he did not depict these countries, but, by a wholly natural mental transposition, he coloured with his memories the eternal regret of " elsewhere " that was to be his constant companion, like a sorrowful burden upon the most disquieted, the most ardent, and the most coldly passionate soul hitherto encountered in French poetry.

Scarcely can a few poems of the *Fleurs du Mal* be attributed, exactly and in their entirety, to the memories of this journey, but its influence is everywhere in the warm perfume of these exotic countries that returns constantly as a reminder. They are not the flowers of our country, whose scent he loves to breathe, but strange perfumes from distant scenes.

It is not that he preferred them, or would have been happy to return to those regions. There is no evidence that, during his life, he ever had the intention of doing so. He seems to have been much more attached to the modern manifestations of artistic life in his day. But, in his mind abandoned to dreams, these distant countries locate the aspirations that he is not destined to realise.

There exists, in truth, a word that contains the entire soul of Baudelaire, his whole genius and his whole heart, a word that he seldom utters, but which resides at the root of his desires, his regrets and his lassitudes ; a word which constitutes the framework of his writings, which explains his curiosity, directs his criticism, and has made of this man the

N

most surprising intelligence of all French poets. That word is : nostalgia.

The dictionaries explain nostalgia as a melancholy caused by the lively desire to revisit the homeland, such as is colloquially termed home-sickness. Baudelaire's nostalgia cannot be defined otherwise, but one must reflect that in him this desire to revisit the homeland carried with it the certainty of never attaining to satisfaction or appeasement, for he was one of those minds whose home is not earthly, and who seek in activity only an appeasement or a distraction. Baudelaire is certainly not alone in having borne the heavy burden of this malady of the Infinite. But in his works it has achieved an expression of such grandeur and beauty that it seems little probable that they will ever be surpassed. He will be found confessing to it on every page of his works. In the *Fleurs du Mal* there are scarcely any poems that do not reveal it. It forms their sorrow-laden texture and their bitter obsession.

He dreams unceasingly of departures for indefinite countries where the tedium of his ever-dissatisfied soul could find distraction. He dreams unceasingly of countries from which he appears to himself to be returning, so clearly do they assume to his acute senses the sharp relief of real life ; and, constantly oscillating between a regret and a desire, he can no longer find repose but in an insatiable curiosity interspersed with solitary, deceptive, and melancholy dreaming.

The soul of romanticism, exasperated with sentimentality, had experienced the bitterness of vague disquiet, attaining to suicide in Werther; but Baudelaire reveals with magic grandeur the new form of human discontent. The mind acquires a greater value in its sickness. It is in his intelligence that this man suffers, as the romantics had suffered from the deceptions of their sentimental imaginations.

Thence comes it that the bitterness of Baudelaire always preserves a restraint that forbids him all exaltation. There had been others before him who felt this insufficiency of the mind in the presence of its own questions, but the proud yet pitiable sensitiveness of Baudelaire gave to all this an entirely different form. Without respite a new vision constantly imposed itself on his outlook. Without respite this ardent spirit, nourished on beauty, thought to discover the object of a definite attachment, but all his scruples arose in unison to lessen every joy and deprive him of all rest.

He has stated it himself with great precision in one of his prose-poems, *Les Vocations :* " It has often seemed to me that my pleasure would be to proceed straight ahead, without knowing whither, without anyone being concerned, and constantly to see new countries. I am never at ease anywhere, and I believe that I would always be better elsewhere than where I am."

And in another entitled *N'importe où hors du monde* he says : " It seems to me that I should always be at ease there where I am not, and this question of removal is one that I am constantly debating with my soul."

Others would have lyrically cursed life and destiny, and sighed abundantly over such original sin : but that is where the art of Baudelaire reveals a character that is peculiarly its own.

As has been accurately said by Jules Laforgue : " He was the first to express himself in a restrained confessional-tone without assuming an air of in- spiration." [1] Where others would assuredly have uttered imprecations, he has only an ironic word, in which the wound in his heart is the more powerfully revealed. From childhood he preserved to an unimaginable degree the modesty of his sentiments. The love of solitude never left him, as if the presence of another might have disturbed his dream of " elsewhere." Yet his heart was full of tenderness held in check. His letters reveal it in spite of himself. This man, athirst for solitude, was still more athirst for a presence that might have brought calm to his mind and have appeased the unceasing disquiet of his heart.

And this man, to whose name was attached a legendary reputation for perversity, reveals an unimaginable ingenuousness of heart. This braggart of vice reveals in his letters sentiments which he endeavoured all his life to dissimulate, through a haunting solicitude to escape from indiscretions, the more to enjoy the charm of solitude. A thousand instances betray that his impassive exterior veiled a strange internal disquiet, in a singular association that gives him the sorrowful aspect of Hamlet. All

[1] Jules Laforgue : *Mélanges Posthumes*. Published by the *Mercure de France*.

the evidence of contemporaries who were in close
touch with him, Gautier, Banville, Flaubert, and
many others, is in accord. It shows him moderate
in the choice of words, always conforming to the
strictest politeness, expressing paradoxical ideas in
a tone of great simplicity, and with a somewhat
British coldness. His gestures were rare and
moderate, and as if always controlled by a precise
determination.

No other writer was more aloof from artistic
Bohemia than Baudelaire. None other preserved a
greater self-control. All his life he endeavoured to
recover himself, to struggle against the forces that
cast his dream adrift. He had the desire to recreate
his soul, in order to owe it in some measure to himself, and to feel that he belonged to himself. But
his mind was constantly attracted by vain visions,
by insatiable curiosities, and by this splenetic state
of discontent. And it is this confession that is
constantly repeated in his works, with ever the same
nostalgia, in *Les Hiboux*, in the admirable *Cygne*,
and in so many other poems. And who could
suggest nostalgia when speaking of Baudelaire
without the evocative and melancholy title of
L'Invitation au Voyage rising of its own accord to
the lips ?

The whole of nature, all things around Baudelaire,
solicit and invite him to travel towards that country
where " *tout n'est qu'ordre et beauté, luxe calme et
volupté.*" It is a journey without a destination,
that is constantly resumed because it is projected but
never accomplished save in dreams ; and this

Invitation au Voyage returns as a sorrowful echo in his works. Baudelaire has resumed this theme a thousand times. Is it not in the *Invitation au Voyage* of the prose-poems that one finds this sentence : " A musician has written *L'Invitation à la Valse* ; where is he who will compose *L'Invitation au Voyage* " ?

This is an indication revealing his obsession with music, his deep consciousness of the impossibility of better expressing the idea that haunted him save with the help of the evocations of tone. In vain he resumes in words this desire to be elsewhere, which is an obsession for him. He feels that no word will ever express his longing to escape from his world and to tear from it his tenderness in order the better to reveal it whole. He feels that music alone might perhaps advance a little further into the secret avowal of his heart.

Music has not yet seen the birth of a composer whose soul might correspond to that of Baudelaire. Yet some have endeavoured to follow in music the text of Baudelaire's poems.

The contents of these poems are at once ample, strong, and subtle. The music with which they are accompanied runs the risk of detracting from their dignity by overloading them beyond measure, or it threatens to remain far from attaining their subtlety. To realise their essential characteristics, qualities are required similar to those of the mind which composed them.

The lassitude, the gravity tinged with nostalgia, of the mind of Henri Duparc enabled him to evoke with dignity *L'Invitation au Voyage* and *La Vie Antérieure.* How many others have failed !

For inquisitive minds the works of Baudelaire are an inexhaustible source of themes for meditation. In intellectual contents they rank among the most important we possess in France, and if it is true that his poems, especially, are infinite subjects for meditations and dreams, how alluring is also all that portion of his works in which Baudelaire reveals himself as the first, the most alert, and often the most prophetic of our art critics, even were it limited to the long and masterly study of Richard Wagner which he published as far back as 1861.

He was obsessed with everything belonging to this world from which he sought to escape. At his funeral Théodore de Banville rightly said : " He accepted all that is modern man, with his weaknesses, with his morbid grace, and with his helpless aspirations."

No phrase can better sum up Baudelaire : " He accepted all that is modern man." To condense one of the most acute revelations of modern man : he knew all the deceptions, aspirations, nervous disturbances, anxieties, triumphs and failures that may be represented in a sensitive soul of our time. He had so often paused at each of the cross-roads which the modern soul offers and at which the modern soul sometimes hesitates until it can no longer act. Maybe those are happy, and, after all, maybe not, who preserve the serenity of olden times amid such a whirlwind of forces, amid such a tempest of ideas as we are confronted with in our day. It is not a question of unravelling whether this is better or worse, but we shall never prevent a soul athirst for certitude from seeking to inform itself, to revert to principles, to realise the appeasing unity of these raging forces. For in that lies the sole effort and the sole tormented desire of every conscious and meditative soul in our epoch : Unity. It is this " desire for unity " [1] which haunts every mind, exhausts it in the search for links to bind its least thought to the rest of the universe, and leads it to the discovery of new analogies.

" Analogy "—and this is the other pole of Baudelaire's mind. Nostalgia in his inner being ; and analogy for his outlook on the universe—analogy, or, as Baudelaire often uses it, the word of mystics : " correspondence."

Some content themselves with approximations. Their pretended analogies are merely verbal, and dissolve at the breath of time. But others (and these are the fertile minds of a race and an epoch), penetrate words, seize them at the heart, and, in drawing two ideas together with characteristic violence, compel them, in spite of their sometimes contrary design, to enter into the unforeseen plan of a new analogy.

Baudelaire assumes this *rôle*, foresees its scope, indicates some of its paths with the penetration to which he was inclined by his temperament and every attitude of his mind.

If nostalgia is the fundamental theme of his

[1] One may profit by reading on this subject a fine book by Adrien Mithouard, entitled *Le Tourment de l'Unité*.

works, analogy is their constant mode of expression. The intelligence of a mind shows itself in the greater number, appositeness, subtlety, and simultaneous amplitude of the relations it establishes between the elements of its universe. The relations which Baudelaire establishes are infinite. His sensitive soul made him penetrate to the very essence of things. Always eager for definition, he retraced thought, feeling, and life to their sources, which he discovered to be a common source; and his dream, in which the elements of his vision were mingled, revealed to him their mutual correspondence.

This burning desire for unity led him to give it the most perfect literary expression it has yet had since certain poems of Gérard de Nerval, in which there already appears the feeling of mental reservation concerning all things in one. Baudelaire has thrown in this direction a more accurate and comprehensive glance, and it is thus that he has expressed it in his sonnet *Correspondances*, which no longer needs to be quoted, so completely has it become established as a classic, and so often has it provided a theme for artists and critics : a classic sonnet quoted as much in musical works as in books on philosophy, and containing within itself, if not the whole outline of Baudelaire's works, at least the whole form of his art.

Thence have proceeded a thousand preoccupations of contemporary French poetry, for the true disciples of Baudelaire are not those who, like Rollinat and others of his kind, have sought for *macabre* effects which are not in Baudelaire. When

Baudelaire evokes death, it is with profound grandeur and profound bitterness, and as a philosophic rallying theme. The true disciples of Baudelaire are those who have endeavoured to develop and to define the whole art-matter which lies there, the whole of this new aspect which the universe has for the soul that loves meditation and beauty.

Time has brought a revolution from the strict division of styles. The modern soul, urged from all sides, cannot withstand the different currents. The modern soul, in its desire to live with ardour, must see multiple aspects before it. All the dams have burst one after another. The rules of Aristotle are abolished. Poems in set forms have disappeared. Verse itself has become emancipated in turn.

The mind, carried away by the tempestuous desire for unity, has understood that though its aspects be multiple, the essence of all beauty is one, that only the idea is essential, and that in our day the beauty of expression may be equal to formal beauty, revealing the reflection of the soul in the spectacles of the universe.

The time has passed of the simplicity of lines in the Greek conception of beauty. The time has passed of the refined splendour of the Italian renaissance. This age, to a greater degree than its predecessors, is eager to attain to the heart of the mystery, to reach, if not the reason of things, at least the atmosphere of the inner life; and it is this that has yielded for us the moving wealth of essayists, Emerson as well as Novalis, Mallarmé and Meredith, Jules Laforgue or Villiers de l'Isle-Adam.

All these minds, with or after Baudelaire, have felt, and we feel after them, how thin are the partitions that separate things and ideas, how thoughts are merged in one great stream, and how near the mode of expression of one art is to that of another.

Les couleurs, les parfums, et les sons se répondent.

In the soul of him who yields to dreamy nostalgia, landscapes have no deciding lines, and faces are vague as those of the old pastels, or of paintings blackened with age. Nostalgia has none other theme than that of regret, but the regret itself is vague, for it is regret not of a definite object but of an aggregate of a thousand indistinct objects which appear merged in the distance.

Baudelaire did not regret Calcutta more than Réunion, but the imaginary transposition of these places. He did not regret these places themselves, but their analogies in his soul. In this we discover that the two elements in the soul of Baudelaire are not elements of discord or of strife, but elements consequent one upon the other. If the nostalgia is vague, if it is in ignorance of the definite point, whether that which arouses it is less the object itself than the radiations of which it is the centre, it is for this reason that it is conducive to the creation of new analogies. By the bonds of vague memory the mind links itself to places, to landscapes, to faces, to the atmosphere. The nostalgic mind listens to these confused suggestions which become as the utterances of the Pythia, and present to the mind the nearest, yet the most diverse, meanings. They are the material of dreams, and of dreams that are scarcely definite. And what art but music can express the indefiniteness of the nostalgic dream ? What art but music can lay claim to the greatest power of suggestive analogy, a power greater than that of words, though their evocative quality be that of the words of Baudelaire ?

It is to music, always and without ceasing, that the soul and the thought of Baudelaire incline. The word " music " occurs frequently in his writings, but its essence is everywhere in them, for its essence consists in nostalgia, transposition, unutterable relations, and analogies.

The works of Verlaine are musical, but melodically rather than profoundly. Those of Baudelaire are musical to their very heart. That is the secret of their wealth and of their magic power.

On reading once again the poems of Baudelaire, however often one may have read them before, one suddenly discovers in them a new indication. It is a new dream-portal opened to a multitude of associations. We experience a similar sensation on hearing again a sonata by Beethoven, a song by Schumann, or a passage from *Tristan*, however dear to our hearts and familiar to our minds ; but it means that a new correspondence has been effected between the musical theme and our present mood.

For the rest, Baudelaire's preoccupation with music betrays itself in a thousand places : this astonishing phrase in the *Confiteor de l'Artiste*:

" *Toutes ces choses pensent, mais musicalement,*" or the sonnet, *La Musique,* which opens thus: " *La musique souvent me prend comme une mer.*"

One might quote a score of penetrating passages from his remarkable essay on Richard Wagner, written when none of the musicians appeared to foresee the importance of the Wagnerian will-power and its desire to merge all the arts in the lyric drama.

This essay on Wagner has not been read sufficiently. In it one may find this : " It would be truly surprising if sound were not capable of suggesting colour, if colours could not give the idea of a melody, and if sound and colour were inadequate to express ideas, for things have ever found expression in reciprocal analogies since that day when God put forth the world as a complex and indivisible whole."

Therein resides the very kernel of his æsthetic. Therein lies the great strength that animates and stirs his writings, making of them the unprecedented evidence of a sensibility that is at once grand and acute, a sensibility that is in the highest degree musical, and concerned with the mystery of the intangible.

Music, the consolation of all nostalgia, and the atmosphere wherein dwell all analogies, is unceasingly and invisibly present in him. Think what separates the admirable Alfred de Vigny, for example, from Baudelaire, despite their belonging to the same intellectual family : one remains a sensitive thinker, but a descriptive thinker ; the other has the gift of evocation. He came at a time when the symphony was beginning to offer to French minds the inexhaustible resources of its moving symbolism.

Baudelaire stands for the first occurrence in French poetry of deep preoccupation with the essence of music. It was not only that the coincidence of events drew him in this direction, but that his entire nature led him thither. And the musical resources of Baudelairian sensibility are not yet exhausted.

They have tempted more than one composer. Whilst some, like Henri Duparc, were suggesting in music the melancholy and ardent gravity of Baudelaire's thought, others sought to translate into music his sense of infinite subtleties, and his taste for refinement. Thus Claude Debussy in his *Cinq Poèmes* evokes with minute precision the thoughts that dwell beyond the landscape, and the atmosphere of mystery in which floats the intimacy of his mind. With a care corresponding to that of the poet, he seeks to liberate in the musical picture all the emotional elements it contains. In *Le Jet d'Eau*, in *La Mort des Amants*, and in the grave and touching *Recueillement* he has succeeded in not betraying the proud and yet fraternal sensibility of the poet who had, in a higher degree than any other, the sorrowful privilege of understanding the modern soul, and of penetrating the human soul to its uttermost depths ; those depths where, perhaps some day, all our nostalgia will find appeasement, and where all analogies will be combined—the uttermost depths of the human soul where all is music and poetry.

(1908)

PAUL VERLAINE AND THE MUSICIANS

De la musique avant toute chose,
De la musique encore et toujours.

VERLAINE himself gives us the above advice, and in that order. How, in truth, could one better honour him, or better speak of him, than with the music of his own verse, or with the music for which his poems provided some of our greatest modern musicians with subjects?

Verlaine is not of those of whom one may speak in scholastic terms. He does not lend himself to the support of a thesis. One cannot find in him an austere subject. Yet a grave subject is one that enlists our affections, sometimes bitter, yet often sweet. Verlaine is not one of those geniuses before whom all sentiment, even pride, necessarily bows. He was a man, simply a man, at once inferior and superior to every one of us. One may remain in complete ignorance of him, but if some day he has touched us we shall be unable to forget him, and inevitably compelled to love him.

" De la musique avant toute chose,
De la musique encore et toujours."

Thus speaks Verlaine, and it is his entire soul. Nothing is more characteristic of his writings, and nothing expresses more fully their essence. " *De la musique avant toute chose*," but he is not con-cerned here with what is commonly termed the music of verse, euphony, eurhythmic, the sense of metre and of stresses. He is concerned here with the very nature of music. The writing of Verlaine is of the same essential quality as music, and infinitely closer to that art than to literature.

Words are in truth full of deceit and trickery. Some men are skilled in imparting to them a thousand different meanings. Words are of a soft and resisting substance, stretched and moulded to suit the moment. They are what one makes of them, when they are not what they make of themselves. They are hypocrites of whom one will never be master, and Æsop's apologue on the tongue, with a hundred others, is irrefutable evidence of it.

But music is inevitably fated to be sincere. There is no deceitful music, though it is true that there is good and bad music. It is the means of giving artistic expression to an emotion or a sensation. Its essence, which is also the principal element in the writing of Verlaine, is sincerity. It expresses pain or tenderness, fear or anger, but always it speaks with the voice of the soul, and not merely with words that proceed only from the lips.

From the moment that music exists, good or bad, it is sincere ; and thus it is with Verlaine : perverse or mystical, it is the sincere cry of his soul, or of his body.

They are thus similar, music and Verlaine. They are sincere, without intention, without consciousness, because it must be so. It is a command of the life universal which they obey. That is why they are merged in life, which they express with unequalled intensity. That is why the poems of Verlaine are not mere words, but songs, wails, sighs, shouts, curses, or groans.

Verlaine was, and remains, a singular being whose personality has always adhered so closely to his work that death itself could not separate them. He came at a time when the prevailing idea of a poet was that of a man inspired, a man whose every action appeared superior to those of average humanity. Verlaine is a man who aspires, who endeavours and who fails, who wills and no longer dares, who rises and falls, and who sings his aspirations and even his failures. He is an unfortunate passer-by, something like a street-singer who might sing the *lieder* of Schumann. He is a vagabond with genius.

Even in his earliest poems one meets with this singular mixture of tenderness and savage humour, this drifting in style of which one cannot well say whether it is due more to neglect than intention ; this balance which unceasingly oscillates between the joyful freshness of childhood and the lassitude of a morose mind. Even then he gave proof of a personal use of familiar terms, of everyday words to which, by means of his marvellous musical instinct, he gave a new meaning, or at least the impression of one.

At the time when Verlaine was writing his poems, French music was extricating itself with difficulty from the domination of the theatre. Whether the official musicians applied themselves to the trills and runs of Italian opera, or the more modern among them felt the influence of Wagner's genius heavily upon them, the forces of musical France were employed almost exclusively in dramatic music, or concerned in fostering fashionable virtuosity.

O

Schubert had been dead for forty years, and Schumann for ten, but the French public was still ignorant of either, and musicians seemed unaware of the almost infinite paths indicated by their works. Both the French composers of the period, and the public, had been too long engrossed in the external aspects of the stage, and in mere effect, without troubling to establish unity between the poetic and musical intentions. They thus conspired together to retard the development of a musical type that ranks among the most admirable and the most alluring : the *lied* or art-song.

At that time, towards 1866, nearly all the most venturesome among young French musicians, for instance, Saint-Saëns, were addicted to the ornamental aria whenever it was a question of " setting words to music," as the saying is. Let us turn for preference even to the declamatory style which mars the few songs which Wagner composed to French words in his earliest days, and most of those of Berlioz.

This new poet, this refined and discreet sensibility, this delicate art of infinite nuance, had need of a musician with personality, an artist who, reared upon Schumann and Schubert and retaining only their essential nature and the form of their prosody, if one may thus describe it, would express, within the restricted and intimate frame of the *lied* (art-song), an equivalent sensibility, original and wholly French, uniting the same qualities of depth and refinement. That was the *rôle* of Gabriel Fauré.

It will never be sufficiently repeated to what

extent one must, in the history of the French art-
song, consider the works of Fauré simultaneously as
a starting-point, and as one of its most admirable
achievements. It is, in fact, to Gabriel Fauré,
concurrently with Castillon, Henri Duparc, and René
Lenormand, that we are indebted for the first
attempts in this musical art-form, which was new to
France and was destined to attain immediately to
a rare degree of perfection.

The history of the *lied* in France, even if considered only in its musical aspect, could not be
written omitting the name and the works of Paul
Verlaine. Certainly this poet did not alone determine the remarkable movement that took place from
1867 onwards to transform the romantic type of
song into the *lied* as we understand that form to-day,
but the publication of *Fêtes Galantes, La Bonne
Chanson, Romances sans Paroles*, placed at the
disposal of musicians a series of excellently suitable
poems, suitable in a unique degree to this form of
song, and they perhaps hastened its definite con-
stitution. In any case, Gabriel Fauré was one of the
first to realise the degree in which these poems were
susceptible to music.

For thirty years numerous musicians have sought
themes in Verlaine, and yet, despite the best of them,
such as Debussy, Ernest Chausson, and Charles
Bordes, Fauré has remained the true musician for
Verlaine in all his more intimate aspects. Gabriel
Fauré's Verlaine songs are many. The musician
has taken texts from nearly every volume of the
poet. He has even commented almost in its

entirety the collection *La Bonne Chanson*, and
always with a choice of harmony, and a depth and
clarity of expression, that equal the poem itself in
the intelligence of the commentary.

It is only to superficial minds that Verlaine's
writing can appear monotonous and attenuated. In
truth there is none more diverse nor more complete.
A false conception of greatness may have led some
to believe that, with him, it is a matter only of small
impressions and minute notes. In point of fact,
there are pages of Verlaine which attain to the very
essence of the heart, and their musical nature is
exhaled quite naturally.

It is strange that the author who has had the
most influence on the musical movement of his day,
or at least whose works are the most intimately
linked with it, was precisely the author least concerned with it. Musical productivity has not been
for Verlaine what it was for Mallarmé, or especially
Baudelaire, or for Villiers de l'Isle-Adam. The
vagabond and Bohemian existence led by the poet
did not draw him into circles where efforts were
being made for the revival of French music. He
would have been estranged equally by the "good
form" that prevailed there, and by the discussions
of musical technique.

There would, moreover, have been no advantage
to Verlaine in becoming interested in musical
technique. He carried in his mind the feeling of
the mysterious domain which is only half evoked by
words, and which overflows their rigid shapes.

Indefinite line, evasive and seemingly careless

expression through which one divines, in spite of all, the anxious modern sensibility, are modes that are naturally suited to musical commentary ; and thus it seems in certain of Verlaine's poems, when set to music, as if the composer had done no more than underline the inflections of the poet's thought, and follow its subtle and floating outline.

There is more than one example to be found in the works of Gabriel Fauré. Verlaine's sensibility has no more faithful translator. The French grace of Fauré is always happily combined with Verlaine wherever the poet is ingenuously charming, with a slight touch of melancholy that increases the attraction.

Thus certain songs of Fauré have justly become classics, such as *Clair de Lune*, in which the melody, tenderly languishing as the listless lines of the poet, is underlined with a minuet motif that effaces itself, reappears, and vanishes once more, following the slightest intentions of the poet and continuing them amid the delightful mystery that music imparts to the evocations suggested by it. But it is chiefly in that admirable epithalamium, *La Bonne Chanson*, that the meeting of musician and poet is happiest. After *La Bonne Chanson*, Verlaine was perhaps to have finer utterances, revolts of the heart or revolts of the flesh, but he was never to make better songs, or songs that expressed or gave more consolation, or that were simpler or sweeter. And in the language used by Verlaine, which is so devoid of artifice, this acquires the value of confidences in which we recognise the expression of all our best wishes.

There, more than anywhere, the soul of Verlaine,
and the atmosphere in which it floats, are musical.
There, more than anywhere, the poems are songs
which of their own accord call for music; and if the
music they attracted to themselves was not always
worthy of them, at least some of it is of sufficient
excellence to obliterate the mediocre.   Where the
soul of Verlaine charms us, it has found none more
worthy to evoke it in music than Gabriel Fauré, and
where this charm attains to the profound purity ever
met with in French poetry, it has no more worthy
fraternity of soul than with Ernest Chausson.   This
composer's modesty, and his sometimes over-
scrupulous conscience, did not permit him to offer
his work often enough in his lifetime to the admiration which it deserved.   Since, in 1899, a brutal and
stupid accident came to rob the cause of French
music of his life, his fame grows and rises, a slight
compensation for the void created by his death.

It is not that Verlaine has a large share in the
copious song-production of Chausson, but the two
poems he has set, *Apaisement* and *Ecoutez la chanson
bien douce*, give the standard of his unequalled
purity.

The little poem to which Ernest Chausson gave
the title of *Apaisement*, and which opens with " *La
lune blanche . . .*" has tempted many musicians.
None has rendered its exquisite melancholy or its
simple, ineffable purity more successfully than in
Apaisement, where the melodic phrase unfolds itself
to an accompaniment made of a few sweet chords
whose modulation is mysteriously resolved.

La Bonne Chanson represented but a brief spell of calm in the vagabond soul of Verlaine. He then turned his back for ever on the tranquil happiness of a peaceful life and entered upon the lamentable existence of a vagabond, wandering, at the call of a torturing curiosity, in *"chemins perfides, douloureusement incertains,"* from which he henceforth lacked will-power to redeem himself. As he then became, so he was to remain all his life. Henceforth the blue sky is darkened. It will ever be clouded, though with occasional breaks, as in *Sagesse*. Always there will be this combination of purity in his work, and pollution in his life.

One need have no fear of belittling Verlaine's work by relating his pitiable life, without attempting to conceal its repellence. His work remains for all to enjoy its grandeur and charm. But truly, what a powerful gift this wretch, this jailbird, this drunkard, must have received from nature to have been able, throughout his orgies, his vileness, and his misery, to retain his ingenuousness of heart, his delicacy of vision, and his impulsive power ! Who could have withstood such a life ? He must have received as his portion that which Catholics mean when they speak of " grace."

This grace was Music ; it is the great purifier, the great consoler, as Schopenhauer and Nietzsche themselves have asserted. All the best that was in Verlaine, that which appeals to us when we love him, was Music. It was the natural expression of his heart, the safeguard of his genius, and the guardian of his fame. As he drifts at the mercy of circumstances, of his desires, his curiosities, his passions, and his vices, he sings ; and these songs become *Romances sans paroles, Jadis et naguère, Parallèlement, Liturgies intimes.* He sings his heart's regrets. He sings his heart's desires. He sings the landscapes in which his heart seeks eternally an unattainable peace. He sets a personal stamp on these landscapes, and the memories he has bequeathed us of them are not the least interesting portions of his works. It is even by these, especially, that some of Verlaine's composers have been attracted, among them Gustave Charpentier and particularly Claude Debussy.

There is formed in Debussy's music an admirable alliance between the sense of reality and the sense of mystery. Its character is at once legendary and authentic. It is both material and ethereal. It is deeply intellectual, and yet deeply sensuous. It could not apply itself with more complete fitness than to this poet.

There is here no question of evenly decorative music. With Verlaine, as with Debussy, the landscapes are not separated from the soul that considers them and animates them. *Spleen, L'Ombre des arbres dans la rivière,* and the ending of *Chevaux de bois* prove to what degree sensibility plays a part in their suggestions. It could not be otherwise in the songs of one of the most sensitive musicians that ever lived. Claude Debussy has long held in affection the charming poet of the *Fêtes galantes,* and of the *Ariettes oubliées.* Some ten songs exist to establish this special love which has persisted from his earliest compositions to his last works. Beyond the charm and the purity of Verlaine, or rather apart from these, but side by side with them, he has a picturesque side, careless and witty, that also deserved to be translated into music. There is in *Le Faune*, in *Chevaux de bois*, in *Fantoches*, a rhythmic side, of which Claude Debussy has been able to take lasting advantage. Some there have been who have reproached Verlaine's poetry with a certain monotony. There will ever be some to speak of things before they have even considered them; but to convince oneself of the injustice of the charge one need only read the three sets of songs in which Debussy has illustrated Verlaine's sensibility. One will see at once how varied are the nuances. In the droll gait of *Fantoches*, the hammered rhythm of *Chevaux de bois*, the dull tambourines of *Le Faune*, the admirably languorous phrases of *C'est l'extase*, and the melancholy theme of *Spleen* or of *Il pleure dans mon cœur*, we shall find most of the diverse aspects of Verlaine's feeling, and the proof of their engaging variety. The extraordinary musical intelligence that presided over all Claude Debussy's musical illustrations, of which *Pelléas et Mélisande* is not the least, has manifested itself in these songs with singular felicity. There is not an indifferent page in them, and, even among those who know how to enjoy the rare quality of Verlaine's verse by itself, there are many who cannot fail to recognise that this music has but further enhanced the charm and the feeling that words are incapable of transcending.

The feeling of freshness that ever characterised Verlaine's personality and his work was destined to assert itself even more fully in a unique book which is perhaps the most beautiful he wrote, in pages which constitute the most splendid confession of Catholic faith that French literature possesses since its very origin. Such ingenuousness, such simplicity in faith, and such sincerity in expression, have no equivalent in French literature, and can only be compared with the works of César Franck.

What a distance there is between the healthy life of the one and the faun-like existence of the other ! Yet here Franck meets with Verlaine.

The saint meets with the sinner on the path of belief.   What matters that the one may have come to it from the high planes of grandeur, dignity, and silent sacrifice, and that only an impulsive enthusiasm enabled the other to reach it, coming from marshes and muddy brooks, his flesh torn by the bushes and thorns of the road !   They have met at the sacred fount.   Each, for the moment, will look no longer behind him, but towards the immaculate snows where dwell the elect, and, as there falls upon them the twilight of a century of which *Le Génie du Christianisme* [1] was the dazzling dawn, they both proffer, with the same gesture of brotherly kindliness, the urns from which believers may quaff the inexhaustible and incomparable water, where even those who are unable to admit its efficaciousness, are yet able to quench their thirst in its limpid freshness.

[1] By Chateaubriand.

We may surely regret that we do not possess a
song by César Franck to a poem of Verlaine. Their
meeting could not have failed to be felicitous.
Failing Franck, two of his pupils have sought there,
and not in vain, themes suited to their glowing
spirituality : Chausson, and Charles Bordes, the
delightful composer whose works are too little
known because this art-propagator who devoted
himself to music and gave up all his life to it, whilst
claiming justice for the past, for his contemporaries,
or for to-morrow, forgot only to ask a share of it
himself in his own lifetime.   Yet his songs to poems
by Verlaine would alone suffice to secure him a
delicately beautiful place among the poet's
musicians.

Day by day the musical settings of Verlaine
increase (more or less worthily, it must be admitted).
Certain clear spaces of the soul, certain impulses,
seem necessarily to attract the notation of harmonies
and of melodic line.

In all its forms music is the soul of Verlaine's
poetry, and that is why he has been, and will be,
passionately beloved of musicians.   Fauré, Lenormand, Debussy, Charpentier, Bordes, Sylvio Lazzari,
Ravel, Sévérac, and yet others, have mingled their
voices with that of the vagabond singer.

For so large a number of musicians to have been
attracted by his poems, for such intimate cohesion
to exist between words and music in their songs, it
was truly necessary for him to be one of themselves,
for the genius of the composer alone could not have
sufficed.

French poetry and French music are indissolubly linked at the heart of Verlaine's poetry, and around his works, with as close a bond as that which unites German poetry and German music in Heine and Schumann.

The name of Paul Verlaine could not remain associated only on the covers of songs with those of the best among contemporary French musicians. A study of French music of the present could not without injustice omit the part that his presence has involuntarily played in the development of the French *lied*, and none who enjoy music may henceforth forget that it is in the garden of Paul Verlaine that have grown some of the most beautiful flowers of French musical sentiment.

OPERATIC POETS

THE French Academy is endowed with a Soussaye prize destined as reward for the best operatic libretto in prose or verse submitted to its judgment. There is good reason to wager that this prize is devoted to crowning the worst possible work ; one of those that perpetuate the dramatic commonplaces, and jingle qualities of which we have already only too copious evidence. To speak the truth, what have academic prizes to do with the destinies of literature ?   There are few academicians who can perceive the musical possibilities of verse or prose, and the musical requisites of an operatic libretto.

Nevertheless, if there be a period when the

operatic libretto should, and might, recover the dignity that belonged to it in the days of Quinault,[1] is it not the period when music and literature have for thirty years and more become mutually penetrated, and have borrowed means of expression each from the other ? Whilst the symphonic poem and the " programme " were invading musical preoccupations, poets, in disjointing the romantic alexandrine, were bringing into existence a free verse that, in the hands of a Régnier, a Gustave Kahn, a Viélé-Griffin, a Verhaeren, or a Mauclair, acquired diversity of inflection and revealed unsuspected qualities.

It is true that operatic poets have rare opportunities of meeting with a musician. The best of the composers of our day devote only a small proportion of their works to opera. As against one Étranger,[2] one Pelléas, one Pénélope, one Ariane et Barbe Bleue, how many . . . Far too many ! Moreover, writers still regard the operatic libretto as a negligible and uninteresting literary type, whether it be that they do not care to study it deeply, in spite of their musical taste, or that they hold the share of the librettist to be too secondary.

Yet it will escape nobody that the efforts made by Verlaine, and the poets who succeeded him, to render verse more supple, to accentuate its lyrical elements, and deliver poetry from simple, hollow rhetoric, have aided the marvellous efflorescence of French song since Fauré, Chabrier, Chausson,

[1] 1635-1688, the poet of Lulli's operas.
[2] Opera by Vincent d'Indy.

Duparc, or Debussy. It is impossible to-day to have accurate views on the evolution of French music in the last quarter of a century if one is not sufficiently informed of the evolution of French literature in the same period. They hold together more closely than ever, and they can only have profited from their union. Musical works such as the *Chansons de Bilitis*, *Pelléas et Mélisande*, the *Prélude à l'après-midi d'un Faune*, as well as the *Chanson Perpetuelle* or *Les Heures*, are not born from the momentary meeting of a musician and a poet, but from the deep and constant intimacy between music and literature.

Apart from one or two exceptions, the whole of the best literature of this period is plunged in music, whether we speak of prose-writers like André Gide or Suarès, or of poets like Henri de Régnier or Camille Mauclair. There have been failures enough, stifled or notorious, to give proof of the emptiness of the operatic style as manufactured in the workshops of licensed librettists. Only the monstrous " oratorio " book is more ridiculous. Present-day composers, or at least those of them who have some personality, have taken the course of preparing their libretto themselves, whether they invent one altogether, or reduce and transform to their convenience, in accordance with the musical requirements, the works to which they feel attracted.

It is, in truth, from the operatic libretto that must come the solution of the opera problem. It is the librettists, or rather the operatic poets, who will bring about the escape from a style whose conventions have reached the limits of tediousness.

Perhaps the success of the Russian ballets and the intelligent decorative and literary efforts of the *Théâtre des Arts* offer the indication that we must resume the path of the old *opéra à divertissements* as it was in the time of Lulli, Rameau, and Campra, or possibly modified to suit our present requirements, but carrying with it a similar union of music, poetry, and dancing.

Opera has scarcely to do with classical tragedy, from which our modern intentions are somewhat removed, and the æsthetic of the open-air theatre, suited to outbursts and roars, does not accord with the present tendencies of French music, which are infinitely more decorative and more subtle.

The operatic poet who will create the desired libretto will not be he who will seek to impose upon the music a libretto in contradiction to its tendencies, but he who, having lived in the musical atmosphere, having entered into relations with the best minds in that art, will have grasped its aspirations, whilst, at the same time, being sufficiently master of the verbal harmonies of the language to provide the composer with a text that is strictly " musicable."

There is scarcely the possibility of a libretto to-day apart from free verse or rhythmic prose. The necessary incidence of the rhyme and the regular subdivision of the alexandrine cannot easily accord with the music of our day. It was thus in the time of Lulli, and Quinault had understood it. The perusal of his operatic poems still holds charming and delightful moments in store for inquiring readers.

The question of the operatic libretto cannot be a secondary one for those who are passionately devoted to music. It is the good librettists, the true operatic poets, who will restore the interest of music-lovers in an art-form that sometimes, and at long intervals, is connected with music by works like *Boris Godunoff* or *Pelléas et Mélisande*.

There are surely in these days some young poets, skilled in the use of the delicate and supple instrument of free verse, who at the same time do not tire of rehearing the *Images*, *Estampes*, *Miroirs* or *Gaspard de la Nuit*, and who follow with equal diligence the independent exhibitions of decorative art, and the Russian ballets. It is these who will give back to opera its old-time dignity, whether by giving it a new strength, or by restoring its lost qualities of a fairy-play in sound and sentiment.

Which among them desires to be the saviour of opera ? Quinault is to one style what Racine is to another. Such writers as Louis Gallet, or Henri Cain, are scarcely the equals of Campistron.[1]

But when this operatic poet has written the pure and beautiful libretto for which we are waiting, let him not send it to the academicians, but take it to a true musician. It will be at least a saving of time.

(1911)

[1] 1656-1723.

VI
THREE PERFORMERS

THE PERFORMER

IF one truly loves music, it is difficult sometimes not to execrate the performers, for the purposes to which they apply it are often worse than base. They employ it solely to gather the applause of the crowd, without giving a thought to the dignity of the works, or to their own.

Some attain to dazzling positions, attract eager multitudes, and are overwhelmed with the weight of floral tributes and eulogy, and, during their whole lives, they have ministered only to their own appetite for praise.

One could cite to-day more than one whose fame deserves nothing more than a shrug of the shoulders. Showmen and posers abound, and the refuges of music have a mouldy odour of the Lower Empire ! Some, whose conscience admits of no compromise, have set themselves to denounce this mob. Less fortunate in some of its other manifestations, the vigorous perspicacity of Romain Rolland has depicted this *Market-place* [1] in sincere and vivid colours, and one can read again and again with rugged enjoyment the courageous writings of Nin directed against the mountebanks and their retinue.

Among musical performers in France, few are to be found who have not to blush for some of their

---

[1] In *Jean-Christophe*.

past or present programmes. Arrangements, and
other evils of virtuosity, find most of them always
ready to sacrifice with a light heart all care for their
musical salvation.

If, for the present, programmes have been a little
purified, there still remains much to be done, and
one must not measure one's language or be at all
moderate when an instrumentalist reduces his art
to the most sordid trickery. The more famous the
clown, the more he must be attacked, though he be
given the rank of a minister or an ambassador. Let
him put up his trestles at the suitable spot, in the
circus or in the market-place of a county town.
Each thing in its place, and especially music.

For many years these people have been met with
at every cross-road, sniffing whence blows the wind,
raking up as many followers as they can, and in constant pursuit of music to do it some injury. By every
means, and especially by that method which is most
dangerous because apparently the gentlest, their
coalition opposes the purging of programmes and
the education of the public. Between them and
ourselves war must be constant and without quarter·
without pity, without considerations of philan-
thropy, or of pauper relief.

If we have any influence, let us use it to defend
those who do their duty. Let us bar the way of
those who flatter the basest instincts of the musical
crowd. Let us fight all " tenors," and all those
who are pleased to believe that the works were
made to serve them, whereas their sole duty is to
be the humble and respectful servants of the works.

There is a form of musical criticism that has made itself the handmaiden of these parvenus. Such people go together as the fox and the crow : we are not dwellers in those woods.

Critics and performers alike, we owe it to ourselves to endeavour to understand and to express ; and the least creative artist takes precedence of us, for he furnishes the opportunity of a new vibration, since he brings to the world a little of real life, whilst we critics and performers give only its reflection.

The Press distributes epithets to-day with shameful prodigality, and these performers are well suited with praise on the level of their mediocre character. It is for who shall be the most talented, the most delectable, the most eminent. When one sports stripes one cannot assume too many. To read the journals which print these encomiums, one would imagine oneself to be in some nigger republic. There are none but are generals. They are all the grandsons of General Boom.

Sometimes their grotesque antics are diverting. If one were to listen to peaceful people, one would leave these puppets alone; but they take up, in truth, too much room. These marionettes are not worth the string they dance on, and there is no need to tolerate their usurpation. If truly the function of the critic is to discover values and not mere appearances, he should fulfil it with dignity.

Let us stand by the word of Chamfort : [1] " If one has the lantern of Diogenes one must also have his stick."

[1] 1741-1794.

Fortunate are we when the spectacle is so lofty and dignified that the stick only serves us to hang the lantern upon it and throw light upon a worthy subject, to its fullest extent.

RICARDO VIÑES

Even if Ricardo Viñes were an imperfect pianist, the part he plays in modern music would still remain an admirable one. But, in addition, he is thoroughly competent in all that he does. One is so accustomed to see him make light of difficulties, store up without effort the most forbidding pages, lend himself with an inexhaustible good grace to all musical experiments, that one ends by losing sight of the particularly exquisite aspect of such a personality. Yet, without detracting from other pianists who are entitled to our sympathy, we must recognise that none has accomplished a more ungrateful task, contributed more lively enthusiasm, or given more proofs of an assured taste, in spite of all and of everyone. And none, in our day, and in the musical sphere, has lived in such constant heroism.

Perhaps this heroism is less visible to-day, since those on whose behalf he has fought have now acquired celebrity. But, fifteen years ago, who would have ventured to present to the public the works of Debussy or Ravel and incurred the risk of compromising his career in the attempt ? One must recall the hisses that greeted Viñes when he interpreted, for the first time, Maurice Ravel's *Miroirs*. As he was then, so he is to-day : in ambush behind his moustache, careless of the smiles of the so-called *connaisseurs*, he pursues, calmly and without advertisement, his patient and assured fight to impose that which is worthy.

Whilst others were employed in spreading their monster posters throughout the world, and securing, on the basis of safe works, a tumultuous celebrity, Viñes, hailing from Spain, while still a mere youth, took up in turn the defence of the modern French, Russian, and Spanish Schools with profound intelligence and warm affection.

A considerable number of works will have known for many years no other interpreter than Viñes, and the young pianists who have since followed in his footsteps are well aware that his was the more difficult task. If they do not know it, or give it a thought, it is expedient for us to repeat it to them.

He has been indefatigable, and he is still sought whenever a new work is to be presented. He does not think to-day, any more than he did yesterday, that he has the right to deny his services to a work of value. He puts as much heart into studying it, understanding it, and defending it, as if it were a question of the work of a genius of the past ; and sometimes it reveals itself as the work of a new genius of to-day.

In vain, after having disdained this " pianist of the modern school," they have sought to confine his taste to one style of music. He loves both the old and the new, the serious and the amusing, and does

not think it beneath his dignity to lend the support
of his hands to the affectedly humorous pieces of
Erik Satie.

How often was he in request to learn from manu-
script, in a few days or hours, a complex and
refractory work ! At the stated time, unfailingly,
he was at the piano, appearing and disappearing,
hiding himself behind the author, asking for more
works, and, between two orchestral concerts,
labouring persistently at the music of an obscure
composer.

Rarely has such a task been accomplished with
more sustained modesty. He has performed it with
so much personal effacement that one would regard
his modesty as exaggerated, did one not find therein
ground for loving him the more.

Though he has devoted himself, more than most,
to difficult music, he has retained no trace of the
virtuoso in the objectionable sense of the word.
How many, in his place, would have claimed merit
for having interpreted compositions of such difficulty ! When he is playing, one does not give it a
thought. Without preliminaries or display he
presents the work. It is only right that one should
remember the prodigy of this great ease in performance. Often one does not even remark it. That
is as such a pianist would wish.

For the young French School he has been even
more than an interpreter : truly an incentive, and
a collaborator. We should probably be the poorer
by several of the best piano works if he had not been
there to play them, eager for new music, and if the

composers had not felt at their side his unrivalled memory, his irresistible hands, and the enthusiasm behind his smile.

The musical life of Ricardo Viñes would furnish sufficient activity for more than one man. Yet this pianist will be seen at picture galleries, private views, and exhibitions ; he reads the Fathers of the Church ; knows by heart Villièrs de l'Isle-Adam, Mallarmé, Claudel, and Jammes ; is familiar with the best English books, and does not forget, moreover, that he is a Spaniard.

He is one of the few in our time to restore the full dignity of the performer. He is aware how much modesty and self-respect, how much sacrifice and unwavering love, are involved in this function, and, at the same time, he contrives to avoid assuming the attitude of the prophet or the schoolmaster.

It would seem to be a mere diversion for him. He plays with his piano, and his only care is to evoke or transmit according to the intentions of the creators.

For that there is no need to imitate the platform-pounders ; a little quiet suffices him : intimacy, and a few friends gathered round the piano. Or, in the concert hall, with the orchestra, to embroider with meticulous fingers the iridescent phantasy of Rimsky or of Liapounoff.

He is not an ivory-tamer, like this or that pianist of our acquaintance. When Viñes plays Chopin's *Barcarolle*, Fauré's *Nocturne in A flat*, or Albeniz's *Triana*, our heart is in his hands. When he sets Ravel's *Jeux d'Eau* rippling or Debussy's *Poissons d'Or* flashing their colours for our pleasure, the whole picture is reproduced in its lights and shades, in its nimbleness and its splendour. And when, with an assumed seriousness that is betrayed by the joy in his eyes, he interprets the verve of Chabrier, or the smile of Satie, we are unable to withstand the lure of this pleasant adventure.

He can assume all shapes. There are few more varied than he. It is not yet sufficiently known that he is not merely a pianist, but one of the greatest artists of our times. He has conquered for French music the best minds from North and South. He carries on a peaceful struggle with the uncomprehending and the timid, wherever an alert musician calls him. In our day there is none who has made known more music or better.

His repertory is prodigious. Perhaps no pianist has ever had one like it. One wonders how he has been able even to read all the music that he plays from memory. He always appears as if he had plenty of time. He finds enough of it to indicate to you in which corner of Paris you may see a new pastel by Redon, or a sumptuous Monticelli. He is seen at all concerts. He reveals new things to us in the poets we know the best. Coming from a recital at which he has just performed a considerable feat of memory, he goes, his arm linked in that of a friend, to recite a few hundred lines of Baudelaire or Verlaine. He devotes himself to everything without languor. He is never tired of admiring something. There is nothing of which he is ignorant. We may chat with him for hours and forget that he is a pianist. He knows all that is worth knowing in order to give music higher rank than that of a mere craft.

We owe it to him that we know and love many things. He is an example of the rare but necessary virtues one must have if one wishes to serve music. We have not the right to remain in ignorance of one who can give so much pleasure and is able to convince the most sceptical that no compromise is forced upon anyone who really knows the value of art.

Ricardo Viñes is a peaceful prodigy.

JANE BATHORI-ENGEL

WHO has not heard Jane Bathori sing has not penetrated French song. There is no art more true or more discreetly human. It is the perfection of proportion. We can trace in her art all the French qualities, and, whatever we may derive from it, these touch us more deeply than all transports, however passionate

There are few in these days to equal her in restoring to song all its intimate values. In listening to her it is not of herself or of her voice that we think, but of what she suggests through the music. Only afterwards can we measure the extent to which art is concealed by art itself.

Who will ever sing like Bathori the *Chansons de Bilitis* and *Le Promenoir des Deux Amants*? Who will ever be able to put so much freshness, ingenuousness, intelligence, and heart into them?

As regards the heart, there may be some who will perhaps contest this, as it is necessary for most people that the whole body be agitated. For them, if there be no fury or heart-rending cries, it is not true that the heart is speaking. So much the worse for them if they are hard of hearing. It is yet another French quality to understand what is half said.

I listen to her singing the complaint of Mélisande or the youthful and fresh joy of *La Bonne Chanson*, and I feel thoroughly that it is our heart that speaks in her voice. I know, further, when hearing her sing Chabrier or Ravel, that none other has done so with more wit, more verve, or more impulse in combination with all the requisite tact.

As compared with so many unfaithful interpretations, what rare magic resides in such an incantation! But still more remarkable is the presence of such an interpreter simultaneously with such an opportunity.

She is modern French song incarnate. For more than ten years she has offered to all our young composers of any merit the calm assurance of a perfect collaboration.

Who would have cared to play that *rôle*, apart from the resources it demands? It needs more than mere talent, and more than mere intelligence. It also requires courage. In these days perhaps only Ricardo Viñes has displayed more courage.[1]

---

[1] Let us recall that for more than twenty years Emile Engel has displayed the same courage, the same art, and the same ardour in the service of French music,

That does not lead to the noisy fame of virtuosity, the vast posters, or the triumphal successes, but it gains on behalf of yet unrecognised works interest, a following, and finally an ever-increasing enthusiasm.

We ought to do homage to artists of such a rare type, and, without employing in reference to them the hollow eulogies of unabashed advertisement, it is mere justice if we no longer keep for our inner tribunal the recognition of the beauty that we owe to them.

The first time that I heard Jane Bathori was on an afternoon in October, in the early days of the autumn Salon, in a small, rather uncomfortable hall where nothing lent itself to enjoyment, and where even the sparseness of the audience added an indescribable lassitude.

Not even the name of the singer was known to me. The memory of what she sang that day has left me, but not the strange and deep impression she made of an art till then unheard of, and yet ardently longed for. Others had succeeded in charming us by the mere beauty of tone, the broad dignity of line, or the passionate richness of some tragic outburst. But who was to interpret at last in a French manner all that our favourite poets evoked in us : the beloved Baudelaire poems read in the evening calm, those of Verlaine as fresh as the smiles of children, and all that intimacy of the soul, this " chamber-music " for voice and heart ? And when would song, emancipated from the theatre, consent to come and speak to us between the four walls of retreats of our lay oratories, during the evenings lit by the firelight glow?

I felt that day that this music had found for itself an incomparable exponent. Since then each hearing has furnished me with more certain proofs. Her art is all of nuances, and cannot be seized by any detail. One is unable to segregate any element that is peculiarly characteristic of it. It is the great quality of true beauty that its ultimate springs defy analysis.

It may well be that extreme penetration enables Jane Bathori to attain to the summit of such an art, that all in it is minutely calculated, that nothing is left to chance. Nevertheless it is impossible to surpass it in naturalness and in that apparent spontaneity which alone has importance for the listener, though it be the fruit of knowledge and diligence.

But, from the outset, the vivacity of her musical sense fully discloses to her the true accent of the most complex works. How often has she not revealed the delicacy of songs whose interpretation, at the cost of inevitable haste, appeared almost as the performance of an impossible wager. Yet she at once brought out all their light and shade, and the full suavity of their nuances.

It is impossible to carry any further simplicity in song, the comprehension of a poem, or the precision of its accents. It works in the truest sense as a charm. One cannot tire of it. When listening to her the man of letters is as satisfied as the musician. Her diction allows nothing to be lost. The bright moments and the shadows are disposed in delightful fashion.

All is there, in right proportion, and this increases the range of a voice which, in another, might perhaps seem weak.

It is in similar terms that was praised, in the eighteenth century the singer Marie Fel, who "created" the works of Rameau, of Jean-Jacques Rousseau, and of Mondonville, and of whom Latour has bequeathed an admirable portrait. She is not without a certain musical affinity with the singer who has "created" the songs of Debussy, Ravel, Roussel, and so many others.

In both are present the same artistic qualities, the same knowledge, a similar inclination towards the newest works that give occasion for discussion, the same vocal simplicity, the same scrupulous care of refinement, and the same absence of display even in the most ardent passion.

In her day Marie Fel was justly named "the Heavenly."

J. JOACHIM NIN

It is rare in our day to meet with a conscience like his, without weakness, and, one might almost say, without hesitations. Its merit is further enhanced by the fact that the dignity of his mind is not associated with any stiffness, and is able at all times to preserve the engaging charm of sincere simplicity. No mind stands more aloof than his from pedantry, and from those immovable dogmas which give to most only the illusion of a right to despise their rivals and their period.

A feeling of freshness is in the atmosphere that constantly surrounds his thoughts, and his whole life is governed solely by the unceasing desire to understand, more fully and more accurately, the spectacle of beauty.

None who have met him can forget the extent to which he was helpful to them, and, in the circumstances, we must restore to that word its full vitality. There are some whose uncertainty concerning the best direction to give to their endeavours found in the spectacle of his actions and writings a peculiar power and the solution of their doubts.

It is a strange power, that of youth, serious and smiling together, full at once of knowledge and of life.   When one considers Joachim Nin's age, one is surprised that he should have such an ascendency over less youthful minds.   But when one draws nearer for a moment to the forms assumed by his thought, one quickly understands the attraction of its purity and its grandeur.   We live in a period in which unreasoning eulogy is cultivated to excess. There is as little moderation in this as in any other matter, and one no longer knows how to express the respect and affection due to those who perpetuate in our day the virtues of a past which may perhaps be imaginary, but whose domain consists for us in its greatest achievements.

Strength of will and sensibility share his mind equally and contribute to establish an unfailing balance. The only enemies he knows are those who introduce into the kingdom of music the methods of mountebanks.

A remarkably gifted pianist, he could, like many others, have aimed at the rewards of virtuosity, and accumulated by means of conjurers' tricks the palms of public appreciation. It needs a soul tempered as steel to resist the attraction of popularity, without weakening at the alluring sound of applause, and without inclining gradually towards the charming social gratifications that fall to a fashionable *virtuoso*.

J. Joachim Nin has always kept before his mind that art is a grave responsibility, and that the mission with which the performer is entrusted enjoins renunciations, strict duties, and continued self-control. Rather than be at the service of crowds and publics, he has employed himself in the service of music.

That is not so common a choice as one might at first suppose. When one examines the lives of performers, when one examines their programmes over a period of some years, it is rare that one fails to find some concession, some avowal of weakness indulged for the satisfaction of the public. If one searches the musical past of Joachim Nin, one will not find in it a single action that is not prompted by a deep love of art, and by disinterested devotion in the cause to which he has vowed his life, his strength and his talent, and to which he has joyfully sacrificed the ephemeral tributes of social favour.

One must have seen Joachim Nin interpret some

Q

old master.   His marble-like features reveal nothing
externally.   There is no exaggerated gesture to
procure substantially the satisfaction of the listener.
All is concentrated, and, behind that immobile
mask, one feels vibrating the respect and enthusiasm
of the performer who is endeavouring to reveal, in
all its authentic, sensitive beauty, the page bequeathed by genius.

His love for French culture and for the expression
of the French race has made him familiar with
French works of the present and the past.   He has
devoted his talent to reviving for us the treasures,
too often despised, of our musical ancestry.[1]

Chambonnières, Couperin, Dandrieu, Daquin, all
our clavecinists of the seventeenth and eighteenth
centuries, have received from him the most truthful
interpretation.

In the course of the programmes which I had the
pleasure of giving with Joachim Nin, I could judge
at leisure of the degree of conscientiousness in his
work.   His concern is not restricted to the written
music, but, with untiring curiosity, he looks all
round it for everything that may determine with
more precision the real atmosphere of the composition.   He knows the lives of the composers, their
thoughts and their circumstances, and everything
that may have influenced the form and the particular tendencies of their minds.   He is interested

[1] We may read again, with added interest, the *Letters from
Berlin*, which Joachim Nin addressed to the *Monde Musical*
from December, 1908, to June, 1909, and in which he defended
the cause of French music with ardour and with much usefulness, on enemy territory.

in the historical surroundings of the work, and its position in space and time. But he does not bring to bear upon it the cold compulsion of a rigid historian. It is living art that draws him, and the past only attracts him that he may again strike from it the spark that formerly lit it and that eternally smoulders under the ashes of unmerited neglect.

The work performed by such a mind is considerable. Thus understood, the preparation of musical works demands unremitting toil, and it would be so easy to avail oneself of science to the detriment of beauty. Joachim Nin considers erudition to be the necessary basis of interpretation, but he then endeavours to conceal it as well as possible in order that the work itself may be allowed to speak with the sole aid of its own beauty, the sole power of its grandeur or its charm.

He has not restricted to the teaching of the piano the noble thoughts with which his mind is obsessed. He has gathered in two booklets *Pour l'Art* and *Idées et Commentaires* the principles of conscience which have always guided his conduct.

The first is a little pamphlet whose success was well merited and which, translated into four languages, has given useful indications, as stated in the dedication, " to performers as they are and as they should be."

" Play for the Muses and not for me," said Antigenidas [1] to one of his pupils who was troubled at the indifference of the crowd. This advice, at once haughty and melancholy, governs all Joachim

---

[1] *A Theban musician.* Val. Max. III., 7.

Nin's activity. As a pianist he is one of the few who truly do honour to an instrument that is ordinarily more propitious to juggling than to confidences. By his actions he justifies his aversion for those who, under the ægis of art, barter both music and themselves.

In these days, which are at once the days of scepticism and of small religions, it is rare that a man dares to risk the isolation of the part played by an apostle. Such a mission is no more enviable than it is envied. The path is adorned for your passage with awkward thorn-bushes. It is so easy to deal out to you, stupidly, its supposed ridicule. It is necessary that you hold yourself equally aloof from the visionary and from levity. You are the butt of the centurion's sarcasm, when not of the drunken helot. You run the risk of becoming elated as much with vanity as with discouragement.

Joachim Nin has successfully escaped one danger and the other. He is not the dupe of his soul, however generous it be. He does not imagine that he can alone contradict the efforts of so many slaves. He knows that to be a free man one must also speak in moderation, though with firmness and with faith.

He has scarcely passed his thirtieth year. He possesses marvellous gifts, an eager curiosity, and a burning capacity for work. He has often known success of the rarest kind. He has every inducement, or at least would have them all if he consented to adopt the customs of performers. Instead of doing so, he is at pains not to captivate. He retires behind the works. He wishes to hear no opinions but theirs. He knows that the ways that captivate the public are sown only with lies. He shakes false idols, not with the fury of the neophyte, but with the smiling ardour of a young sage among too skilful scholars.

Pour l'Art brought him, on the one hand, the sudden expression of reliable friendships and warm affections, but on the other much rancour and much enmity. Scarcely had these subsided when he strove again to renew the struggle, as if he desired to impose upon himself the ransom of his success and of his joys.

Pour l'Art and *Idées et Commentaires* reveal an infinite love of music, a religion that nothing can impair, a feeling composed at once of gravity and of rare exuberance, and an unrelaxing contempt for virtuosity, the idol of the crowd, the mistress of false artists, whose reign has lasted only too long.

That is the rallying point of the varied pages of these works, which follow less a literary plan than a governing moral.

"Let us suppose," says Joachim Nin among other things, " someone who would say that the half of a musician's life ought to be devoted to cultivating his mind by contact with the master-pieces of literature, poetry, and painting ; to becoming acquainted with the great problems of science ; to studying art in all its aspects ; to admiring nature, that unique and divine artist, who paints, sings, models, constructs, rhymes, and dances without end . . . that he ought to do this even at the cost of writing fewer compositions, or allowing a

few wrong notes to slip past in playing. He who
would advocate this would be a madman, a pedant,
a dotard, a dunce, a simpleton . . . or a freak!
Who would care to listen to such insane notions, or
read them? Of course I shall take care not to
utter them. . . . But why must Truth remain
always at the bottom of the well? . . . She is so
beautiful, so beautiful. . . ."

With calm and ironical courage Joachim Nin
denounces the abuses from which suffer together
the works and those who love music with a wise
passion. Even the degree of bitterness that betrays
itself in some of his pronouncements reveals the
deep energy and far-seeing serenity of such a mind.
There is profitable food for reflection in his " ideas
and comments " on *L'Or et L'Art, La Critique, La
Véritable Grandeur, Les Bons Apostats, La Sim-
plicité*, and *L'Imposture*. Yet the word " reflection " must not be allowed to imply here the
suggestion of a somewhat preaching tone, or of a
thirst for dogmatism, but simply the grave fervour
with which a sincere man, and an artist knowing is
art and loving life, has meditated upon certain
subjects.

Each of these short chapters is founded upon a
reference to the past, with a kind of coquetry of
erudition that seems to moderate his apostolic
ardour, and yet only strengthens it by giving it a
more secure foundation. One is thus made to feel
that everything supplies him with a pretext for the
defence of his cause.

" Five or six centuries before Jesus Christ," he

writes, " it was said that the stars were equally
distant one from another, that they revolved round
the earth and that the sun was larger than the
Peloponnesus, and *perhaps* as large as the earth.
But, on the other hand, there was attributed to
music, at this same period, a civilising and educating
power, and a moral influence superior to that
accorded to the other arts.

" To-day we know that the stars are separated
from each other by unequal distances, and that the
spaces dividing them are immense. We know that
their movements are independent of that of the
earth. Finally, we know that the sun is bigger
than the Peloponnesus.

" But we no longer attribute to music the beautiful
virtues which the ancients conceded to it with so
much generosity. . . . And there is cruel irony in
this, for of all the beliefs held in those ancient times,
perhaps the only one that has remained absolutely
true is precisely the one that we have hastened to
consign to the dust-heap. Yet we have found none
better to replace it. Why then renounce it ? "

Joachim Nin can be angry without loss of gravity.
He can mock, but he can also smile, and even his
erudition is to him a pretext the better to smile.
Let one judge of it by this fragment of a chapter
which he aptly entitles " *Les Superflus* " :

" Among the divinities of the Veda, there is one,
Agni, who has the rare good fortune to possess three
legs and seven arms. He is represented to us as
riding upon a he-goat. In course of time this
charming little god might well develop into a

musical divinity, presiding, for instance, over the fulfilment of the type of the perfect *virtuoso* of the ivories, for it is certain that, in a very near future, two hands and two feet will cease to suffice for the imperative demands of the pianistic profession.

" It is said that the need creates the organ, and, to justify this need, we have on the one hand the multiple pedals of the clavecin, a defunct instrument that it is sought to revive by means of wholly modern devices . . . and, on the other, the six keyboards of a strange and complicated piano— the Janko clavier—whose numerous and problematic virtues have been vaunted in periodical literature. Moreover, any self-respecting piano has nowadays three pedals.

" Now the piano is scarcely two centuries old. At the rate of six keyboards and three pedals every two hundred years, and on the assumption that the clavecin will disappear for the second time, weary of the struggle, we shall have in six hundred years— which is really very little—twelve pedals for a piano of twenty-four keyboards, that is to say, enough to drive Agni himself mad in spite of his three legs and his seven arms. We may therefore picture to ourselves . . . with a little imaginative phantasy . . . the silhouette of a pianist in the year 2500. It will be charming.

" I forgot the billy-goat . . . but . . . how can we ever know into what we may develop later on ? Besides, there are nowadays famous pianists who, very comfortably seated upon a chair, play two of Chopin's waltzes in combination. Why not admit that there will be some later on who will be able to play in quadruple octaves Debussy's *Prélude à l'après-midi d'un Faune* astride of a nice clean billy-goat? One feat is as good as another."

The unfortunate, or rather, fortunate, thing about these two books is that one truly cannot speak of them without quoting. Although Nin rejects the suggestion of having written here a book in the ordinary sense in which that word is used, the qualities of thought and soul fully earn the description for this collection of propositions that have sprung from a fervent love of music.

Everything in the book reveals an ardent and active mind, sincere and alive. Everywhere is revealed a man and an artist in close union. Such books are not numerous. They go against so many opinions, avowed or dissembled.

As a pianist he has been, and is still, the most enthusiastic propagator of old French music. He has played it in Germany, in Poland, in Austria, in England, in Spain, in Switzerland, in Belgium, and in France itself, where it was of no less service, and he has restored the freshness of life to numbers of delightful pieces which were undeservedly forgotten.

This needs more than talent. It also needs courage, and that virtue is nowadays somewhat rare in literature and in art.

(1912)

VII
FRENCH MUSIC IN ENGLAND

FRENCH MUSIC IN ENGLAND

WHEN one examines closely the development of present-day French music and its projections into various foreign countries during the past ten years or so, one is not a little surprised to observe that England is precisely the part of Europe where has been manifested the most lively sympathy with even the most recent of our musical works. It is there that the most active and numerous agencies of concerted endeavour in favour of French art have come into being, and it is an endeavour pursued methodically, carrying with it a close study that has proved most fortunate for the establishment of our influence or of our suggestions.

Assuredly the æsthetic effect of our modern musicians has not yet made itself felt as vividly in England as it has proved on the young School of Spanish music, or on the Russian School that has renewed the riches and the courage of the earlier group of the Five;[1] but the aggregate of manifestations and the number of books, essays, and articles devoted to modern French music is more abundant in England than anywhere else. There are even points on which we might, as will be seen later, borrow from England for the better knowledge of our present-day composers.

[1] Balakireff, Cui, Borodin, Musorgsky, and Rimsky-Korsakoff.

There is no question that in England curiosity concerning music is still almost entirely of German origin, and it has even assured to Germany a degree of influence the importance of which has been too little understood.

In consideration of this fact it is important to draw attention to the part that French music may play in the diffusion of ideas in England, and to the position to which it has already attained there ; and to observe how the conditions which governed the emancipation of our contemporary music can contribute to give musical England the national characteristics which it knew in the times of Purcell and Byrd.

Towards 1900 only one kind of music counted in England : German music. At the opera it was Wagner ; at orchestral concerts Beethoven, Brahms, and Wagner ; at chamber-concerts Beethoven, Mozart, and Brahms. To these names French music opposed at that time only those of Gounod, Saint-Saëns, and Massenet, represented by a few songs. To tell the truth, France did not count.

We must add that the Germans had contrived to establish themselves as orchestral players, as professors, and as conductors. German editions of music were the only ones to be met with. The German publishing houses had founded branch establishments in London, which had gradually and entirely monopolised the market. All young English composers and performers, influenced by their teachers, went to Germany to conclude their studies, and returned deeply impressed by the superiority, not only of German music, but of the German conception in its entirety.

Economic reasons and commercial factors were also at work, obviously with still greater power, to penetrate England with the German virus; but so far as intellectual influence is concerned it is beyond all doubt that music, unheeded, has played the preponderating part, whilst few Frenchmen were aware of the importance that such influence assumed and still assumes.

German influence was the better able to make itself felt in England, inasmuch as the way had been prepared for it. It is only recently, for instance, that one could find in certain English musical reviews critics who raised their voices against the excessive share of attention given to Handel, and asserted the rights of true English music against a composer whose incontestable genius remains, in spite of all, more German than British. Under cover of the war, and of the national awakening that it has brought, patriotism has been seen, here as elsewhere, to attain sometimes the limits of exclusive chauvinism, which is more than excusable in the days of direct action which we are traversing. The case of Handel is a fairly striking example of this recent artistic nationalism in a country where, in the sphere of art, foreign influences have hitherto operated with unequalled ease. However completely naturalised he might be as an English composer, Handel none the less implanted firmly in England the German conception of music, and with all the more ease that England failed to oppose it with any serious national work.

The complete absence in England of theatres devoted to opera or *opéra-comique* afforded no opportunity for either Italian or French influence to make itself felt at a time when the musical resources of France and Italy were almost entirely applied to the lyric stage, as was the case during the whole of the early nineteenth century.

Mendelssohn's visits to England, the performance of his oratorios and the melodic quality of his works helped to renew, in favour of this composer, the English sympathies with German music. The place which Mendelssohn occupies in English musical culture is still to-day a matter of surprise for those who have received a Continental musical culture. One can almost state that Mendelssohn often occupies, in the taste of musicians, a superior rank to that of Beethoven himself, or of Mozart.

If the influence of Handel still had a certain grandeur and strength, one may say that Mendelssohn's influence has been one of the most detrimental elements in the formation of English musical taste, by its introduction of a sentimentality that has become more and more insipid. It is in order to react against this excessive sentimentality that the agents of German culture brought into play the works of Brahms, which have acquired in England a domain that is far from having its equivalent in France. One may say, in short, that it is round these three great names, Handel, Mendelssohn, and Brahms, that German musical influence has revolved in England during the nineteenth century. It is not necessary to add that the works of Beethoven, Schumann, and Schubert have played there the same part as in France, and that Wagner inevitably aroused vivid admiration; but, so far as the latter is concerned, the absence until recent years of a theatre where the *Tetralogy* could be given necessarily restricted his influence.

England was a country of choral and organ music. On that side again Germany offered an abundance of oratorios, and inexhaustible resources for organists. Contrary to what happened in France, musical England held completely aloof from the stage. It was therefore quite natural that she should be under the exclusive guidance of Germany, which was for nearly a century the sole sphere of abstract and symphonic music.

A few years will, therefore, not suffice to dream of thwarting a movement of this kind, which has struck its roots so far back. It is not even a question of fighting against a comprehensible respect or taste for the masterpieces of Germany's past. For those who, long before the war, were preoccupied with the question of French culture, the problem was to fight against a certain number of dogmatic ideas imported under cover of this admiration for German classical music, and to uproot from English minds the opinion, almost generally held, that music was a German monopoly.

The proximity of France, the rich unfolding of her musical renascence, and the conditions, political

R

and sentimental, brought about by the *entente cordiale*, combined to facilitate a course of action whose extent is unsuspected by many Frenchmen, and whose consequences may now be met with in England at every step. Whilst securing warm and widespread sympathies for our musical works, it has also led many Englishmen to give more attention to the features of French thought, and to find in them yet deeper grounds for sympathy and affection.

After a long period of efforts, harshly debated and resisted, even in France, by musicians who were too firmly imbued either with the formulas of the musical stage or the teachings of classical music, French music had succeeded in securing a footing by the opening years of this century. Towards 1900 it was beginning to be generally admitted, not only that there existed a school of truly French music, but also that the quality of this numerous, diverse, and distinctive group of composers was quite considerable.

The appearance on the stage of Claude Debussy's *Pelléas et Mélisande* was the first evidence of the crowning of these efforts, and made their existence more patent to the public. But that was only one important event in the admirable efflorescence that yielded in turn the symphonic works of César Franck, Lalo, and d'Indy ; the piano pieces of Chabrier, Debussy, and Ravel ; the chamber-music of Chausson, Fauré, Roussel, and Florent Schmitt, and many other works. This movement continued to progress day by day, unceasingly producing attractive new works, giving proof of the deep vitality of French musical genius, and exciting the curiosity of the most alert minds in other countries.

Until about 1905, with the exception of the efforts of Sir Henry Wood as conductor of the Queen's Hall concerts, and apart from the important position attained by Saint-Saëns in English musical circles, French musical activity was limited to the rare presence in England of a few artists belonging rather to the category of *virtuosi*, seeking much more to bring themselves into prominence than to do service to a real cause, and repeating to the point of satiety the works that were already the most familiar, and generally German.

It was therefore impossible to accomplish interesting results, save by co-ordinating efforts, and establishing collective action, spread over several years, for the purpose of developing methodically among musicians, professional and amateur, a knowledge of our national music. Led by considerations of this kind, and having studied the organisation of similar movements of propaganda in the French provinces, a French 'amateur, then residing in Newcastle, M. T. J. Guéritte, developed the plan of action in Great Britain of the *Société des Concerts Français*, which may claim to have effected, prompted or assisted, directly or indirectly, all that has been done in England for ten years in the sphere of French chamber-music.

The first concert took place in 1907. From that time its activities continued without a break, until interrupted in the second year of the war.

Naturally the principal centre of these activities

was in London, where the Society gave in its own
name thirty concerts (planned as four annually),
and succeeded in assembling gradually a considerable
body of faithful listeners.

Taking into account that decentralisation is much
more pronounced in England than in France, M.
Guéritte undertook to spread his activity throughout
the provinces.   Whenever possible he endeavoured
to keep the *Société des Concerts Français*, so to
speak, behind the scenes, and take advantage of the
existing organisations and societies to interpolate in
their schemes programmes similar to those of the
Société des Concerts Français, and devoted, as the
name indicates, exclusively to French works, old or
modern.

Thanks to this judicious plan, the activity of the
Society spread to the Edinburgh Classical Concert
Society, directed by Mr. James Simpson, to the
Classical Concerts Society of Newcastle, to the
Southport Concerts, the Middlesbrough Union, the
Haslemere Classical Concerts, supplying these
societies with its own artists and programmes, and
thus enabling them to realise the importance of the
latter.

In London the *Société des Concerts Français*
sought to induce the established musical organisations successively to utilise the services of the
artists it brought over from France.   It did not
even hesitate to stand aside in favour of some of
these English societies when it judged that the
interests of French music would be better served by
their organisations.   For instance, it several times

relinquished, in favour, among others, of the Classical Concerts Society, the advantage of giving the first performance in London of certain new works, which the composers had reserved to it. Guided by such principles, whose freedom from self-interest is all too rare, M. Guéritte succeeded little by little in introducing French chamber-music into all the .principal English organisations of this kind, such as the Music Club, Concert-Goers Club, South Place Sunday Concerts, etc.

The Society frequently collaborated in the activities of the Incorporated Society of Musicians, and even lent its artists for one of the latter's annual congresses. When it was not possible to make use of the existing associations, it organised concerts on its own initiative in the provinces, at Bournemouth, Leeds, Sheffield, etc.

When the Society suspended its operations, its record of activity to the end of the year 1915 aggregated to thirty chamber concerts in London, and nine in the provinces, given directly under its own auspices ; and forty-two concerts organised in London and in the provinces for existing societies. In addition, ten lectures were given on modern French music. This represents, therefore, a total of ninety programmes entirely devoted to French music which this Society has prompted in the course of eight years.

Wherever one goes in England to-day one becomes aware that the knowledge of French music of to-day is entirely due to the activities of the *Société des Concerts Français* or its connections.

It should be added that M. Guéritte did not limit his activities to the Society which he had founded. He strove in addition to reach the most advanced teachers in the provinces, in order to keep them informed not only of the Society's plans, but also of new additions to French music. By means of copious private correspondence, he enabled these teachers to become acquainted with the works, facilitated the access to scores and the study of documents necessary to a real knowledge of the question, in case of need even forwarding manuscripts entrusted to him for the purpose by the composers. He thus induced them to use their influence on behalf of our cause by public or private lectures, by including modern French works in their pupils' concerts, thereby accustoming the younger generation in England to a knowledge of the names and works of our most recent composers, their mentalities, and their melodic and harmonic methods.

In this connection may be cited the instance of W. G. Whittaker, professor at Newcastle. Associated with the activities of the Society from its inception, and supplied with information by its founder, he succeeded, by means of systematic courses of lectures with music, in making of Newcastle a centre in which there is an intimate knowledge of modern French music in all its developments. At a meeting in 1916 presided over by Mr. Hadow,[1] the eminent Principal of Armstrong College, I was able to judge on the spot of the peculiarly happy results of this campaign at Newcastle.

[1] Now Sir W. H. Hadow.

The English mind is less quick than the French, but more orderly and more persevering. Its natural inclinations must be taken into account. The French composers were systematically passed in review at these functions, whether they were devoted only to two or three composers, or to a group suited to convey the meaning of a special movement of French music of the past or the present.

The older French music served as a rallying point to which one could refer for evidence that France had an important musical past that was too little appreciated, and for proof of the injustice of the impression, that is too often perpetuated, of a French lack of capacity for music.

It was also a happy inspiration to add to the purely French works those of some composers of other countries, but of French musical training, including Spaniards like Albeniz and Manuel de Falla, Italians like Alfredo Casella, Belgians like Jongen, and others, in order to prove the extent to which French culture is able to assist in the development of the musical propensities of other nationalities.

Side by side with the greatest names of the musical efflorescence of our time, works by younger composers were heard at these concerts, giving proof of individual temperaments, and suited to give an accurate and complete impression of this great movement, inaugurated more than forty years ago, whose development the war has interrupted but not arrested.

One of the features of this propaganda is the fact

that, of the four hundred and seven works which have appeared in its programmes no less than two hundred and forty received their first English performance, and this was the case with many works of outstanding importance for French chamber-music, such as, among others, the *Suite Basque* of Charles Bordes ; the *Concerto* and the two *Quartets* of Ernest Chausson ; the *Quartet*, the *Two Dances*, and most of the piano pieces and songs of Debussy ; the *Poème* of Gabriel Dupont ; the *Trio*, the *Sonata in C*, the *Suite in D*, and the *Chansons et Danses* of Vincent d'Indy ; sonatas by Lekeu, Albéric Magnard, Jongen, and Guy Ropartz ; the *Quintet* and the *Psalm* of Florent Schmitt ; piano pieces and songs by Déodat de Sévérac, etc.

It is easy to realise the educative value of such a movement and the difficulties it surmounted, as the purpose in view was to interest the English public in the unknown works of composers of whose very names it was in ignorance. It must not be forgotten that before the efforts of the *Société des Concerts Français* most of the names we have just enumerated had never appeared in the programme of a chamber concert in England.

The influence and the authority exercised by such an undertaking can be acquired only in course of time, and by the exercise of great taste and judgment on the part of those presiding over its destinies. It is in the highest degree important that only works of real value be given, and that these be assured of an irreproachable interpretation.

Concessions to composers or performers of

mediocre attainments would suffice in a short time to accomplish the moral ruin of such undertakings, especially in a country like England, where critics and professors have an authority in musical matters such as we do not suspect in France.

From its first season the reputation of the *Société des Concerts Français* as a serious movement was established by criticisms whose thoroughness and independence might often serve as a model to our own. It became an accepted principle in the English musical world that every work, even if due to the pen of a French composer who was completely unknown in England, was worth hearing, and deserved attention.

I trust I may be allowed to quote a little incident to show the application with which English critics fulfil their functions. When the *Société des Concerts Français*, in 1907, gave its first concert, two critics representing the most important newspapers asked that they might attend the rehearsal in order to gain a more complete knowledge of the works before recording their impressions. They came to the rehearsal and again to the concert. The compositions were Fauré's *Quartet in C,* and Debussy's *Quartet*. These works, and especially the latter, somewhat upset their previously held notions, based on the German classics. This did not prevent them from devoting to these works articles that were attentive, respectful, and penetrating ; and such instances were multiplied as modern French music made progress in arousing the sympathetic curiosity of the English musical public.

Facilities were granted to English students attending musical institutions such as the Royal Academy of Music, Royal College of Music, Guildhall School of Music, London College of Music, and Royal Normal College of Music for the Blind. Tickets at reduced prices were placed at the disposal of young applicants, and a number of invitations were addressed to each of these great musical institutions.

Gradually excellent interpreters were discovered in the country itself. There are to-day in England many artists who can give admirable performances of French music, thanks to their enthusiasm for it, and to the study of which they have made it the subject.

One may say without exaggeration that in the domain of chamber-music all this has been accomplished on behalf of our art, directly or indirectly, by the *Société des Concerts Français*. It is, however, also necessary to render homage to those who have so long contributed to spread an appreciation of our orchestral works, and to those who to-day carry on the same task in this wider sphere.

It is certain that the personal efforts of Sir Henry Wood at the Queen's Hall Concerts have largely assisted for over twenty years to establish in England the symphonic works of Berlioz, Franck, Charpentier, Debussy, and Vincent d'Indy. Inspired by the very laudable desire to keep abreast of the movement, he refused to limit himself to accepted works, and opened wide the doors to the most debated compositions of the young French

School as he has done also for the Russian School.

Several times he invited the composers themselves to participate in the concerts, from M. Camille Saint-Saëns to M. Claude Debussy, who came twice to conduct his works, in 1908 and 1909, and these visits contributed not a little to the quite special celebrity enjoyed by this composer in England.

However restricted the activities of the lyric stage in England, the operatic seasons at Covent Garden had acquired a merited reputation, and, in the last few years, those organised and directed by Sir Thomas Beecham have given further support to our lyric dramas. In turn *Samson et Dalila*, *Louise*, and *Pelléas et Mélisande* have acquired citizenship in London and helped to spread the impression that, though it does not attain to the dimensions of the Wagnerian conceptions, our lyric stage, nevertheless, is far from negligible.

Ever on the alert for novelty, gifted with a prodigious activity, and ambitious to make his energy felt wherever possible, Sir Thomas Beecham is a man whose musical culture is not German, but, on the contrary, widely European. He has an exact appreciation of French resources ; he knows and loves Russian music from Glinka to Stravinsky ; he desires nothing more ardently than to assist in setting English music free ; and he has around him admirably gifted young composers who inspire the greatest hopes, such as Eugene Goossens, among others. Sir Thomas Beecham was naturally for some time exposed to sarcasm and mockery, but the

English public is beginning now to understand accurately the renovating power of such a man, and, now that the events of the war have intervened and led to a gradual reaction against German productions, this same public has begun to take a more kindly interest in symphonic works which hail from other places than Leipzig, Dresden, or Munich.

It is not within a few years that one may expect to see a complete transformation in a country where German influence was so deep-rooted in all that concerned the art of music, but the purely German element has naturally disappeared from English orchestras, and the influence of conductors like Sir Henry Wood or Sir Thomas Beecham, and of young English composers and performers, may within a short time modify the musical aspect of the country.

The influence of several noted writers has also been of some weight in the spread of French music in England. The visits to England of Mallarmé and Verlaine, and the appreciation of the most polished English literature constantly shown by French writers like Baudelaire, Henri de Régnier, Marcel Schwob, Stuart Merrill, Viélé-Griffin, André Gide, Gabriel Mourey, and Gabriel Sarazin, who praised or translated its best productions, whilst English poets and authors like Swinburne, Meredith, Edmund Gosse, George Moore, Arthur Symons, and W. B. Yeats were constantly affirming their predilection for French culture ;—all these circumstances have collectively created, so to speak, a rich subsoil for the intellectual and artistic intercourse that has since arisen and expanded, whilst the brotherhood of arms was being proved on the battlefield of Flanders and the Somme.

Arthur Symons who, so far back as 1900, devoted a remarkable book to French writers since Gérard de Nerval, entitled *The Symbolist Movement in Literature*, was one of the first to examine the suggestions of modern French music in a series of articles which appeared in the *Saturday Review* during 1907 and 1908. I shall never forget the emotion displayed to me by this subtle poet and penetrating critic after the first performance in England of Chausson's quartet, some ten years ago.

As early as 1907, when there existed as yet in France no book, however concise, on Debussy, the series of " Living Masters of Music " published by John Lane included one devoted to that composer and his music, from the pen of Mrs. Liebich, a writer for the *Musical Standard*.

Authors like George Moore, Bernard Shaw, and Arnold Bennett assiduously attended concerts where new French works were to be heard, and spread around them their appreciation of this music.

A new generation of musical critics commenced to fill the posts formerly occupied by men whose whole artistic culture was of German origin. There is in England a great diversity of natural inclination. A large proportion inclines for ethnic reasons towards Continental culture and, without dreaming of becoming slavishly subservient, is naturally predisposed to understand its forms and its innovations, and to seek in them the reinvigoration of its mind and of its artistic conceptions.

There have been known critics of German training who endeavoured to do justice to French music and who ceased to hold contemptuously aloof. The attitude which formerly prevailed is the more comprehensible if one recalls certain opinions expressed some twenty years ago by some of the most noteworthy French critics.

Mr. Edwin Evans, a man of enthusiastic and courageous spirit, whose knowledge of France and of the French language facilitated his penetration of French music, and who takes a somewhat rare joy in expressing his thoughts without reservation, was the first to take up in London, by means of lectures and articles, the campaign which was then being conducted by M. Guéritte in Newcastle, a coincidence of effort that inevitably brought them into close association when the French organisation removed to London. It was he who lectured at the annual conference of the Incorporated Society of Musicians, referred to above, as well as to the Musical Association and other musical bodies. On the eve of the first performance in England of *Pelléas et Mélisande* he gave, in the hall of the Royal Academy of Music, a lecture on that opera, which was illustrated by Mme. Jane Bathori and M. Emile Engel. It should further be remembered that, feeling the need of reciprocity, he has also given lectures before Parisian audiences on English music, notably one on "Modern British Song." He now writes for several journals, and many of his contributions, particularly to the *English Review*, constitute documents of the foremost importance for the consideration of musical questions in England, besides being written with uncompromising clearness and lively spirit.

Soon Mr. H. C. Colles, whose alert and well-informed mind is animated with youthful vigour, began in the *Times* to do justice to French music, without favour, but with an accurate knowledge of the works. In the *Daily Telegraph* Mr. Robin Legge upheld the cause of French music with a degree of impartiality, method, and logic that one cannot honour too much, and placed it in the sphere of study on an equal footing with other schools.

At the same time the English musical reviews generously opened their columns to articles dealing with diverse aspects of French music and its different forms, particularly the *Musical Times*, *Musical Opinion*, the *Monthly Musical Record*, and the *Music Student*, which, for the first time in England, devoted an entire issue to French music.[1]

The quality of the articles which these critics have devoted, in England, to French music, is often of the highest order. If English criticism lacks the brilliant splendour of French criticism, it often has more depth and more knowledge. It is in any case

---

[1] This account of the spread of French music in England is by no means exhaustive. I have frequently lectured in many parts of England and Wales on French music and have taken part in many concerts devoted to French works, during the last fifteen years; and others have done likewise.

No account either is given of the numerous visits of the organists Alexandre Guilmant and Joseph Bonnet, who have consistently played early and modern French music, or of the propaganda at Manchester by Dr. J. Kendrick Pyne.—EDITOR.

necessarily better adapted to the needs of the British public. Especially during the last ten years it has been a valuable aid to the spread of French musical art in Great Britain.

When one has glanced at musical activity in England during these ten years ; when one has travelled in the country and conversed, as has been my good fortune, with critics, conductors, dealers, amateurs, and writers, one arrives at the conclusion that there is no country in the world where French musical art has met with a more ready acceptance, a more widely-spread or a warmer sympathy.

It would not be a paradox to say that the English taste concerning French music is perhaps more reliable than the idea which the French themselves often form of their own music.   When an Englishman speaks to you of French music, it means that he knows it, and in that case he has cautiously reviewed its elements and is in a position to judge.

This is therefore not merely one of those hurried enthusiasms which afterwards leave no trace, even if they are not exposed to the dangers of unfortunate reactions, but, on the contrary, it is a positive sympathy and admiration, acquired from actual knowledge.   Neither can it be ascribed simply to reflected benevolence born from the contact of *L'Entente Cordiale* and of the military alliance. It is something greater. '

If one reads recently in a London newspaper a letter from a reader protesting against the excessive cult of Handel in England, and demanding the more thorough study of a more truly English tradition, one must not see in the incident simply an instance of exasperated chauvinism. It is one of several indications of the fact that England, after a period of artistic indolence which Germany was only too ready to turn to her advantage, and even helped to maintain, is beginning to become more conscious of herself.

For some years efforts have been made in England to restore to honour the works of Purcell and Byrd. Long-forgotten violin sonatas by Purcell and Babell have been republished. There has been a revival of all that delightful efflorescence of four-part madrigals which would be a charming revelation for France. Composers, feeling their way from the midst of the German classical influence, have tried to emancipate themselves by drawing once more upon the treasure of folk-song that is so abundant in Scotland, Ireland, and Wales. The war has only rendered more appreciable and more necessary a movement that has been in preparation for ten years.

And when the circumstances of this awakening are examined, one finds almost everywhere the incitement imparted by the French conscience and the example given by the emancipation of the modern French School from the trodden paths of classical imitation.

In this respect, as in others, the work of the French musicians has been a work of emancipation. The young English composers who are most convinced of the national needs of English music are also precisely those whose interest in French music is most enthusiastic. They are grateful to it not only for the enjoyment they owe it, but for the hopes it inspires in them for the musical future of their own country.

THE END

INDEX

Æsop, 192
Albeniz, 11, 12, 217, 247
Alembert (d'), 42
Allais (Alphonse), 160
Anglebert (d'), 37
Antigenidas, 227
Aristotle, 186
Auber, 26, 58
Aupick (Colonel), 176

Babell, 257
Bach, 6, 26, 38, 39, 53 54
Bailly, 88
Balakireff, 237
Balzac, 42
Bantock, 11
Banville (Th. de), 90, 181, 183
Bardac (Raoul), 100
Bartok, 11
Bathori-Engel (Jane), 219-223
254
Baudelaire, 78, 79, 80, 117,
134, 135, 136, 137, 171-190,
196, 218, 221, 252
Bédier (Joseph), 96
Beecham (Sir Thomas), 251,
252
Beethoven, 5, 6, 26, 27, 28 31,
54, 126, 152, 188, 238 240,
241
Belleau (Remy), 29
Bellay (Joachim du), 29, 155
Bennett (Arnold), 253
Berger (Rodolphe), 86
Berlioz, 8, 26, 27, 43, 88, 146,
194, 250
Besnard (Albert), 129
Bizet, 28
Blanche (Jacques-Emile), 71

Bordes (Charles), 30, 74, 78,
126, 129, 134, 195, 203, 218
Borodin, 237
Bourges (Elemir), 91
Brahms, 8, 238, 240
Bréville (P de), 78
Bussely, 24
Byrd, 35, 257

Cabezon, 35
Cain (Henri), 208
Campistron, 208
Campra, 207
Caplet, 100, 109
Carpeaux, 143
Carrière, 129
Casella, 14, 247
Castillon, 78, 126, 195
Cézanne, 91
Chabrier, 28, 70, 106, 117 121,
128, 131, 205, 218, 220, 242
Chambonnières, 36, 37, 83, 226
Chamfort, 51, 213
Charpentier (Gustave), 200,
203, 250
Chateaubriand, 202
Chausson, 78 80, 94, 102, 126
127-132, 133, 134, 136, 147,
195, 198, 203, 205, 242, 248,
253
Chevillard, 161
Choiseul-Praslin, 175
Chopin, 53, 56, 62, 69, 98, 217,
232
Claudel (Paul), 217
Colles (H. C.), 255
Comte (Auguste), 20
Corot, 142
Costeley, 94

Couperin, 6, 25, 29, 30, 33, 36, 37, 38-42, 47, 63, 82, 93, 94, 102, 226
Cui, 237

Dalayrac, 106
Dandrieu, 29, 33, 37, 47, 63, 83, 93, 102, 226
Daquin, 33, 47, 94, 226
Debussy, 6, 7, 11, 12, 13, 14, 23, 24, 25, 30, 34, 45, 59, 69-84, 85-96, 100, 101, 103, 105, 107, 126, 131, 136, 142, 145, 147, 150, 153, 154, 162, 163, 164, 167, 190, 195, 200, 201, 203, 206, 214, 217, 223, 233, 242, 248, 249, 250, 251, 253
Degas, 91
Delarue-Mardrus (Mme.), 160
Delius, 11
Diderot, 42, 44
Diderot (Mlle.), 24
Dierx, 177
Dukas (Paul), 13, 14, 30, 59, 91, 133, 137-141, 147, 161
Duparc (Henri), 78, 80, 125, 132-137, 182, 190, 195, 206
Duphly, 25
Dupont (Gabriel), 248
Durand-Ruel, 163

Écorcheville, 38, 39, 42
Elgar, 11
Emerson, 187
Engel, 220, 254
Euripides, 66
Evans (Edwin), 254

Falla (de), 11, 247
Fauré (Gabriel), 12, 62-69, 78, 80, 87, 128, 131, 146, 147, 194, 195, 197, 198, 203, 205, 217, 242, 249
Fel (Marie), 223
Ferrari (Gaudenzio), 10
Flaubert, 181

Fontenay (Abbé de), 38
Franck (César), 6, 27, 55, 93, 98, 101, 123, 124, 126, 128, 130, 133, 202, 203, 242, 250
Franc-Nohain, 109
Frescobaldi, 36

Gallet, 208
Gautier (Th.), 72, 181
Gide (André), 78, 91, 151, 153, 159, 206, 252
Glinka, 251
Gluck, 7, 25, 44, 73
Goethe, 138
Goossens (Eugene), 251
Gosse (Edmund), 252
Goudimel, 102
Gounod, 26, 238
Granados, 11
Grieg, 11, 67, 84
Grimm, 44
Grovlez, 78, 100
Guéritte (T. J.), 243, 244, 245, 246, 254
Guilmant, 30
Guiraud, 73, 90

Hadow (Sir W. H.), 246
Handel, 38, 239, 240, 256
Haydn, 6, 10, 84
Heine, 151, 204
Homer, 66
Houdard de la Mothe, 46

Indy (Vincent d'), 12, 13, 26, 30, 87, 121-127, 133, 134, 136, 145, 147, 242, 248, 250

Jammes (Francis), 72, 158, 217
Jannequin, 102
Jongen (Joseph), 247, 248

Kahn (Gustave), 205
Kodaly, 11

Lacaussade, 177
La Fontaine, 175

Laforgue (Jules), 103, 150, 151, 153, 180, 187
Lahor (Jean), 136
Lalo, 28, 70, 118, 128, 242
Laloy (Louis), 85-96
Landowska (Mme.), 21
Lane (John), 253
Latour, 223
Lazzari, 203
Lebègue, 37
Leconte de Lisle, 136, 177
Le Gallois, 37
Legge (Robin H.), 255
Lekeu, 126, 248
Lenormand, 195, 203, 254
Leoncavallo, 61, 86
Lesueur, 26
Liapounoff, 217
Liebich (Mrs.), 253
Liszt, 6, 26, 27, 69, 84, 98
Louys (P.), 78
Lulli, 13, 24, 40, 42, 45, 207

MAETERLINCK, 79, 129
Magnard (Albéric), 134, 248
Mahler, 10, 12, 81, 84
Maillol (Ar.), 91
Mallarmé, 78, 79, 129, 150, 187, 196, 217, 252
Marie-Antoinette, 25
Marot, 149, 155
Marquet, 91
Mascagni, 86
Massenet, 26, 57-62. 63, 86, 89, 93, 238
Mathias, 161
Mauclair, 129, 205, 206
Mendelssohn, 28, 98, 240
Méreaux, 40
Meredith, 187, 252
Merrill (Stuart), 252
Mersenne, 37
Messager, 87
Meyerbeer, 25, 61, 73 98
Mithouard, 184
Molière, 52
Mondonville, 223
Monet (Cl.), 91

Monsigny, 106
Montaigne, 155
Monteverde, 35
Monticelli, 218
Moore (George), **252, 253**
Moréas, 129
Mourey (Gabriel), 252
Mozart, 6, 10, 53, 58, **152, 238**, 240
Musorgsky, 76, 84, **237**

NERVAL (Gérard de), 150, **185**, 253
Nietzsche, 199
Nin, 211, 223-233
Novalis, 187

PELADAN, 163
Philipp, 161
Pizzetti (Ild.), 86
Poe, 150
Puccini, 61, 86
Purcell, 35, 257

QUINAULT, 205, 207, 208

RACINE, 66, 208
Rameau, 4, 6, 7, 13, 25, 29, 30, 33, 37, 41-47, 67, 70, 82, 84, 93, 102, 106, 207
Ravel, 12, 13, 14, 23, 33, 34, 69, 78, 97-110, 131, 145, 147, 148-155, 161, 167, 203, 214, 215, 217, 220, 223, 242
Redon (Odilon), 129, 218
Régnier (Henri de), 72, 78, 95, 160, 205, 206, 252
Renard (Jules), 151
Renoir, 91
Reyer, 26
Rimsky-Korsakoff, **12, 217**, 237
Ritter (William), 10
Rodin, 91
Roger-Ducasse, 12, 69, 100, 105, 109
Rolland (Romain), 3, 4, 211
Rollinat, 185

Ronsard, 29
Ropartz, 134, 248
Roselli (Cosimo), 10
Rossetti, 79
Rossini, 25, 28, 70, 73, 98
Rouché (Jacques), 13
Rousseau (J.-B.), 45
Rousseau (J.-J.), 223
Roussel, (Albert), 12, 13, 23, 33, 78, 100, 105, 110-114, 141-145, 147, 154, 223, 242
Royer, 25, 47

SAINT-ÉVREMOND, 42
Saint-Saens, 4, 12, 13 26 27, 29, 30, 69, 194, 238, 243, 251
Samain, 143
Sarrazin (Gabriel), 252
Satie, 160-167, 216, 218
Schiller, 122
Schmitt, 12, 23, 69, 78, 100, 103, 145-148, 154, 242, 248
Schopenhauer, 199
Schubert, 6, 26, 62, 84, 194, 241
Schumann, 26, 27, 28, 46, 47, 53, 55, 62, 74, 84, 98, 188, 193, 194, 204, 241
Schwob (Marcel) 252
Sévérac (D. de), 23, 33, 34, 78, 100, 102, 105, 109, 155-159, 203, 248
Sévigné (Mme. de), 40
Shakespeare, 31, 148
Shaw (Bernard), 253
Sibelius, 11
Simpson (James), 244
Sorel (Albert), 160,
Stanford (Sir Charles), 11

Strauss (Richard), 3, 8, 9, 10 11, 12, 27, 81
Stravinsky (Igor), 12, 14, 251
Suarès, 206
Swinburne, 252
Symons (Arthur), 252, 253

TURINA, 11
Turner, 150

UHLAND, 122

VERHAEREN, 205
Verlaine, 78, 79, 80, 188, 191-204, 218, 221, 252
Victoria, 35
Viélé-Griffin, 205, 252
Vigny (Alfred de), 189
Villiers de l'Isle-Adam, 78, 150, 187, 196, 217
Villon, 155
Viñes, 214-219, 220
Voiture, 42
Voltaire, 39, 42, 45

WAGNER, 4, 5, 6, 8, 10, 11 26, 27, 28, 31, 55, 61, 70, 73, 74, 84, 93, 96, 97, 98, 107, 123, 124, 130, 183, 189, 193, 194, 238, 241
Waldteufel, 118
Watteau, 41, 143
Weber, 26
Whittaker (W. G.), 246
Wood (Sir H.), 243, 250, 252

YEATS (W. B.), 252